Fine WoodWorking

Turning Techniques & Projects

From the **Editors of** *Fine Woodworking*

The Taunton Press

The Taunton Press
Inspiration for hands-on living®

THE TAUNTON PRESS, INC.
63 South Main Street, PO Box 5506
Newtown, CT 06470-5506
e-mail: tp@taunton.com

EDITOR: Christina Glennon
COPY EDITOR: Seth Reichgott
INDEXER: Barbara Mortenson
COVER AND INTERIOR DESIGN: carol singer | notice design
LAYOUT: Susan Lampe-Wilson

Fine Woodworking® is a trademark of The Taunton Press, Inc., registered in the U.S. Patent and Trademark Office.

The following names/manufacturers appearing in *Fine Woodworking's Turning Techniques & Projects* are trademarks: Abralon®, Dico®, Lee Valley®, Lin-Speed®, Masonite®, Micro-Mesh®, Minwax®, Plexiglas®, Tormek®, Titebond II®, Tru-Oil®, Watco®, Waterlox®.

Library of Congress Cataloging-in-Publication Data

Turning techniques & projects / editors of Fine Woodworking.
    pages cm
"Compiled from articles that originally appeared in Fine woodworking magazine"--Title page verso.
Includes index.
ISBN 978-1-62113-798-6
1. Woodwork. 2. Turning (Lathe work) I. Fine woodworking. II. Title: Turning techniques and projects.
TT201.T869 2013
684'.08--dc23

Printed in the United States of America
10 9 8 7 6 5 4 3 2 1

This book is compiled from articles that originally appeared in *Fine Woodworking* magazine.
Unless otherwise noted, costs listed were current at the time the article first appeared.

ABOUT YOUR SAFETY: Working wood is inherently dangerous. Using hand or power tools improperly or ignoring safety practices can lead to permanent injury or even death. Don't try to perform operations you learn about here (or elsewhere) unless you're certain they are safe for you. If something about an operation doesn't feel right, don't do it. Look for another way. We want you to enjoy the craft, so please keep safety foremost in your mind whenever you're in the shop.

ACKNOWLEDGMENTS

Special thanks to the authors, editors, art directors, copy editors, and other staff members of *Fine Woodworking* who contributed to the development of the chapters in this book.

Contents

Introduction

More and more people are discovering wood turning, drawn to this fulfilling craft for a variety of reasons. For one, you don't need a big shop to do it. All it takes is a lathe and some way to cut up your rough stock, be that a bandsaw or chainsaw or both. Or you can just buy turning blanks in a wide array of gorgeous woods, ready to go. Second, you get beautiful results fast. Whereas a furniture project might take months, even a beginning turner can make a curvaceous bowl or beautiful platter in an afternoon, from rough blank to final finish. Most important, like any woodcraft, turning is a journey. You can start with pens and other small projects and end up making amazing hollow vessels, or bowls with ornate carving, or a segmented turning built up from an array of precisely sized pieces. Furniture makers love turning too, using the lathe to add beauty to their pieces in the form of ornate spindles and posts and unique knobs and pulls.

Although the craft is growing every day, it is not new to the pages of *Fine Woodworking* magazine. From the beginning, the editors have sought out the best turners and teachers to share their practical tips for success. The special collection you are holding comprises the best articles on wood turning from the last decade. Whether you are wondering which tools and accessories make the most sense or how best to finish your piece, you'll find the answers here. We've included articles on basic techniques for every major turning tool, advice on turning a wide array of furniture parts, plus a host of other functional projects, including vessels, bowls, platters, and more. Enjoy the journey.

—Asa Christiana
Editor, *Fine Woodworking*

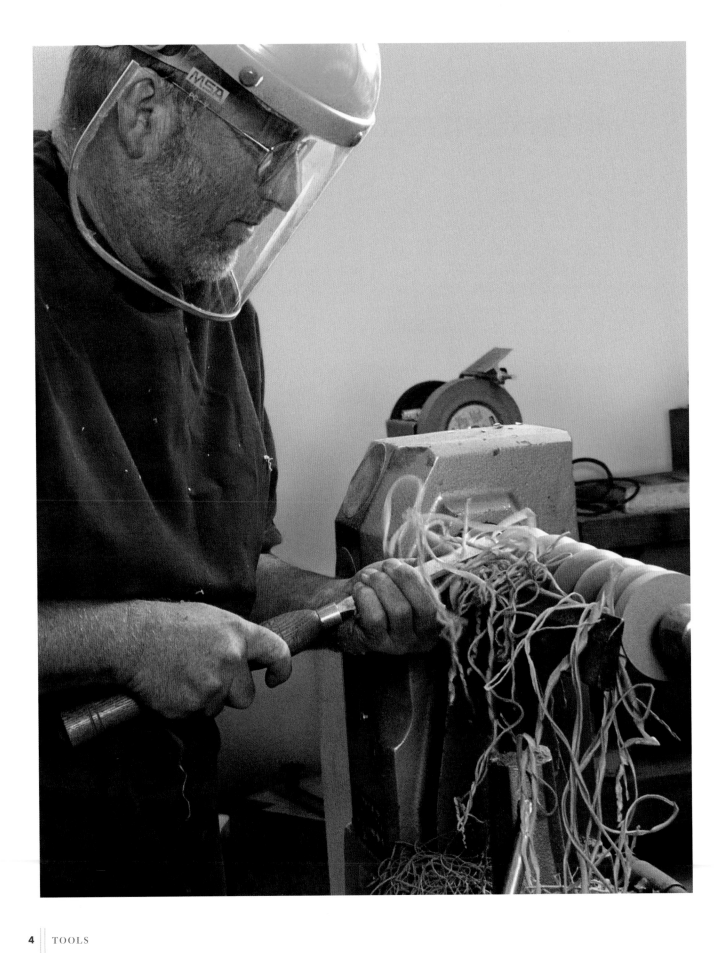

Skew Chisels

RICHARD RAFFAN

Many people buy a lathe with a specific job in mind. Furniture makers want to turn chair stretchers, drawer knobs, or bun feet. Hobbyist woodworkers might want to turn parts for a grandchild's cradle and make bowls. But sadly, many novice turners have their enthusiasm so dampened by the tool catching and digging into the wood and ruining the job that they give up turning almost before they've started.

No matter what you want to turn on your lathe, a few days spent turning grooves and beads between centers using a skew chisel will teach you the basic essentials of turning wood. The exercise will help you develop control and gain a feel for how little force is required to remove wood if a sharp edge is presented at the proper angle. Master the skew chisel, and other turning tools become comparatively easy to use.

Good control comes with practice. Cutting repetitive beads with a skew chisel teaches the basic essentials of turning.

The skew chisel

Skew chisels come in a variety of widths, the most common being ½ in. and ¾ in. They are used primarily for turning beads and round areas on spindle work.

Bevel on both sides

Long corner

Slight radius along edge

Short corner

Edges on short-corner side of chisel are rounded over.

Begin with a sharp tool

I grind a skew chisel with a very slight radius along the edge. Initially this was due to ineptitude, but about 25 years ago I found several advantages to this grind, not least of which is that catches are less severe than when using a traditional straight edge.

Some skew chisels are rounded on the short-corner side so that they slide more readily along the average slightly pitted tool rest. The corners of the chisel can be rounded using a belt or disc sander.

I sharpen my chisels using either an electric grinder or a belt sander. My grinder has two wheels—36-grit and 80-grit. Use silicon-carbide wheels when sharpening high-speed-steel lathe tools. A grinder will put a concave or hollow-ground bevel on the tool. My belt sander is equipped with a 100-grit belt and will produce a convex bevel. Whichever method you use, don't grind a secondary bevel; it will make the tool difficult to control. Grind the tool on both sides and remove the burr with a benchstone.

Practice on scrap or fresh cuttings

A construction site can provide plenty of acceptable lumber for practice exercises. Framing-lumber cutoffs may be had for the asking. Wood destined for the fireplace is also suitable. Choose straight-grained wood about as long as your tool rest. Adjust the tool rest to about center height and orient the stock so that the grain is parallel to the lathe's axis. Before turning on the lathe, spin the stock by hand to see that it clears the tool rest. Set the lathe speed from 1,500 rpm to 2,000 rpm. And don't forget to wear a face shield. Use a gouge, and turn the blanks into cylinders. (On small-section squares you can complete the entire exercise using just the skew chisel.)

Cut a row of evenly spaced grooves

Turning grooves develops fine tool control. You need to pin the tool firmly to the rest with the long point down, then pivot the long point into the wood so that it enters the wood through an arc (see the photos on the facing page).

You can use either an underhand grip or an overhand grip (see the photos at right). I prefer an underhand grip: I hook the forefinger of my left hand under the tool rest, which allows me to pull the chisel firmly to the rest so it cannot easily move either sideways or forward as the point of the skew enters the wood. Other turners prefer an overhand grip, where the fingers are wrapped over the chisel's shank and the heel of the hand leans against the tool rest. Don't push the tool forward as you would a pool cue. The idea is to align the bevel in the direction you want to cut, then pivot the tool into the wood on that line. Start by bringing the long point into the center of your groove 90 degrees to the axis. Then cut in from either side to widen the groove.

You don't need to move your body very much or switch your grip during the cut. Swing your lower hand (the one gripping

Two ways to hold the tool. There are two basic grips that may be used with the skew chisel. Try them both, and pick the one that gives you the most control. Whichever you choose, the tool addresses the stock in the same manner.

Underhand grip. The forward hand grips the shank from underneath, with the forefinger hooked under the tool rest.

Overhand grip. The forward hand wraps around the top of the shank, and the tool rest supports the heel of the hand.

the chisel handle) through a small arc and roll the tool, first to one side, then to the other. The tool requires only the slightest movement to make the cut. The bevel should not contact the wood on this cut. Only the point should contact the wood. If any portion of the cutting edge other than the point makes contact with the stock, you'll have a classic spiral catch, where the tool suddenly digs in. Use the upper hand (the one nearest the tool rest) to keep the tool firmly planted on the rest.

Wider beads are easier to turn than narrow ones, so begin by spacing the grooves about 1½ in. to 2 in. apart. Resist cutting two grooves and then making a bead right away. Get on top of one technique before moving on to the next. Ideally, you should turn several dozen grooves on a number of spindles before attempting beads.

Now it's time for the beads

Bring the skew chisel to the wood with the long corner up and with the tool shank 90 degrees to the axis. This cut is made by rolling the tool with the lower hand while the upper hand (on the rest) ensures the edge doesn't kick back as it keeps the tool pinned firmly to the rest. This grip works well cutting to the right because the thumb provides pressure high up the blade. But you can see that if this grip is adapted to cut to the left, the thumb now acts as a fulcrum, and there's no stabilizing pressure to guard against a kickback at the top of the tool. Catches are much more likely.

In general, an overhand grip, with your fingers hooked over the blade, gives you more control when cutting beads, although you cannot see what's happening as well as when using the underhand grip. Whichever grip you use, the motion to cut a bead must be smooth and without pause. It should take only a second or two to roll one half of a

Groove technique. Begin with a turned cylinder of wood, and pencil in the location of the grooves. Start with the skew chisel on the tool rest with the long point facing down and the edge perpendicular to the axis of rotation. To start the cut, swing the tool in an arc into the workpiece. Don't push it as you would a pool cue.

 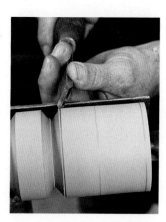

Next, rotate the tool slightly to widen the V-cut. Let the point of the long corner of the skew chisel do all the work. Don't move your body or switch the grip.

What you want to avoid. If any portion of the skew's edge other than the point makes contact with the stock, a classic catch is the result.

bead. Always start at the fattest portion of the bead (see the photos on p. 8).

I prefer a slicing cut, using the leading portion of the edge just behind the short corner, but you need a very firm grip on the tool to avoid catches. You may, however, cut

Handling thin stock

When cutting beads on delicate stock, support the workpiece from behind with one hand (note thumb against side of tool) and move the other hand farther up on the tool handle.

any irregularities. You'll need to learn both techniques if you are going to turn any end grain, as on a drawer knob or similar chuck-mounted project.

As you work toward center with the long corner up, it can be difficult to see the cut proceeding. So at that point, withdraw the tool, flip it over, and work with the long corner down, again ensuring that only the bevel side contacts the wood.

Once you have made one set of grooves or beads, continue practicing by reducing the diameter to a smooth cylinder so that you can begin the process all over again. As the spindle becomes thinner, it will flex unless your cuts become lighter or you use your fingers to equalize the pressure of the tool against the wood. If your fingers get too hot, you are clearly pushing too hard.

using the point of the short corner, keeping the edge clear where only the bevel side contacts the wood as the point shapes the bead. This latter approach is less prone to catches, and the finish off the tool is more than adequate. Although the work surface won't be as smooth as with the slicing cut, a dab of 120-grit paper will remove

With these exercises you'll soon be turning very slim spindles, at which time most other aspects of wood turning will seem comparatively simple, and big, fat spindles a dolly—that's Aussie, for very easy.

Bead technique. Whether you choose an overhand or underhand grip, the movement of the tool is the same. Begin by placing the tool's bevel against the rotating work. The short corner of the tip faces in the direction of cut.

Roll with it. Rotate the tool toward the groove with the forward hand.

Smooth operator. Stop the rotation once the tool has reached 90 degrees and the edge is vertical and facing the groove. The entire movement should be smooth and take only a couple of seconds.

Scrapers

ERNIE CONOVER

Although much turning instruction is devoted to gouge and chisel technique, the scraper is given short shrift—some turners even think there is shame in scraping. This is a pity, because the lowly scraper is a highly useful tool that can get jobs done when gouges and chisels can't.

In faceplate work, for example, it takes a lot of practice before you can fair a perfect curve with a bowl gouge. But even in the hands of a novice, a scraper can smooth both the interior and exterior surfaces of vessels. If fairing a perfect curve is hard, turning a tabletop perfectly flat with a bowl gouge is even harder. Here again, a simple scraper will leave a flat surface every time. Finally, a scraper is the only tool that can cut to the very close tolerances needed when fitting jam chucks or fitting the lid to a turned box.

Scrapers are inherently more forgiving than gouges and chisels because they cut differently. Spindle gouges will cut a bit more or less aggressively in harder and softer parts of a blank. Bowl gouges suffer greatly from this phenomenon, as there is a large difference in the tool's ability to attack end-grain and face-grain areas as the bowl spins. In part, this is because the bevel of the gouge often rides against the surface being turned. On a scraper, the only point in contact with the wood is the burr doing the cutting, so in effect a scraper will machine wood to perfect concentricity. Also, because they are held at a downward angle, scrapers are far less prone to catching and marring the wood. In this chapter, I'll share the mysteries of scraping and bust some of the myths.

All scrapers cut with a burr

To understand how a turning scraper works, examine the simple card scraper. After raising a burr by burnishing, you tilt the card scraper forward until the burr begins to cut. It leaves pronounced, wispy-thin shavings but does not remove much material with each pass, so it is easy to control. The downside is that scrapers dull quickly, for they have to be

How to prepare a scraper. To achieve a more favorable burr angle, turning scrapers have a relief angle ground to about 15 degrees. When the 15-degree bevel reaches the tip of the tool, the burr starts to form.

Make a dome scraper. Swing the tool in an arc of about 150 degrees, maintaining contact with the wheel at all times. With the burr raised, you are ready to put the scraper to work.

A variety of profiles, but all work the same way

Scrapers remove small amounts of wood at a time in a very controlled fashion, making them easy to use. And they can be ground to almost any profile for a wide variety of tasks. Like a card scraper, a turning scraper cuts with a burr and needs to be angled correctly to cut properly.

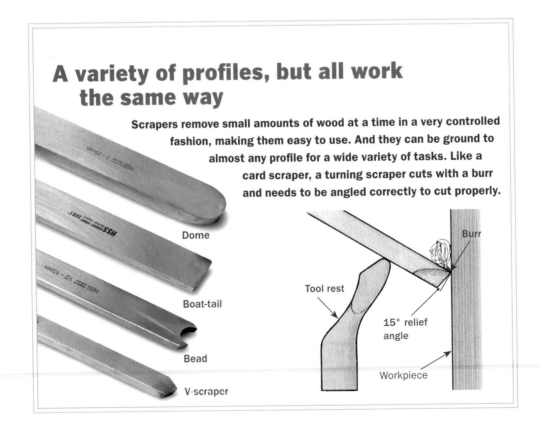

Dome

Boat-tail

Bead

V-scraper

Burr

Tool rest

15° relief angle

Workpiece

Use a burnisher for high-speed steel. On high-speed steel, it is hard to raise a large burr on the grinder. Instead, use a jig with a carbide cone, levering the scraper against a steel pin. If the scraper is thicker than the height of the cone, as shown, place the tool upside down.

Keep grinding to raise a burr

Once the relief angle has been ground, keep grinding at the same angle to raise a burr or renew it in the future. Feel the edge to check when the burr is formed.

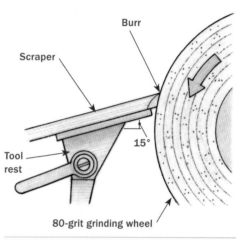

Burr

Scraper

Tool rest

15°

80-grit grinding wheel

softer than other cutting tools to facilitate burnishing.

A turning scraper also uses a tiny burr to cut the wood and is angled forward (downward, actually, on the lathe) to cut successfully. However, there are notable differences with the card scraper: To thin the edge so that a burr can be more easily raised, a 15-degree relief angle is ground under the cutting edge. This increases its usefulness, particularly on the outside of bowls or at a shoulder in spindle turning.

Another difference is that forming the burr on a turning scraper is mostly done with a grinder. About an 80-grit wheel does the task nicely; a good-size adjustable tool rest on your grinder is a big help. The trick is to start moving the scraper as you touch the wheel and to keep it flat on the rest throughout the process. This gives a nicely faired curve on the edge. Once you've ground the relief angle (in the process also raising a burr), if you keep the tool rest at that angle, resharpening and creating a fresh burr takes only seconds. Grinding forms a burr at both the top and

the bottom edges of the scraper, but only the top edge is used.

Like the card scraper, turning scrapers also can be burnished. First, you grind the scraper to the desired shape and then use a sharpening stone to smooth the top edge—what will be the burred edge—and the relief bevel. The idea is to make the top and bevel form a smooth, uniform corner. Because most scrapers are made from high-speed steel, using a regular burnisher will require a lot of force and quite a few passes. A faster method is to use the shaft of a solid carbide router bit, wrapping the cutting surfaces of the bit with duct tape for safety.

You also can buy a dedicated carbide burnisher from Lee Valley®, which has a steel-pin fulcrum point used to lever the edge of the scraper against a carbide cone with sufficient force to roll a burr (see the photo above). The tool is designed to be used with the burr facing up, but if your scraper is thicker than the height of the cone you can use it with the burr facedown. Make sure to keep the tip of the scraper off the base of the

Use a large dome scraper for bowls. It is very difficult to get a smooth surface using a bowl gouge. But a scraper, taking light cuts, can leave the surface of a bowl so smooth that it needs very little sanding.

Another angle. Near the lip of the bowl, instead of using the tip of the scraper and angling the tool nearly parallel to the tool rest, you can tilt the scraper on the tool rest until you find the optimum angle for the burr on the side of the scraper.

fixture. The size of the burr depends on the pressure applied, but in general it is larger and steeper than that made on a grinder, so the tool must be used at a steeper downhill angle. I burnish my large high-speed-steel scrapers for bowl work, and grind all of my small scrapers for more delicate work.

Hold it gently and take a light cut

Your first scraper should be a large dome scraper, at least 1 in. wide, the thicker and heavier the better. They are great for faceplate work, especially bowls. I like a dome shape that is a perfect radius, and I increase and decrease this radius to meet the needs of the bowl I am turning.

Because the scraper is pointed downhill so that the burr drags, the tool rest needs to be raised slightly from the height used for most gouge work. All scrapers have a sweet downhill angle at which the burr cuts best, and finding this angle is the key to success. How much you raise the tool rest depends on the diameter of the piece and how the burr was formed. The trick is to have the scraper contact the work on the centerline at the sweet angle, where it will always be kicked away from the work by problematic spots such as knots.

Stay above centerline inside bowls

The scraper needs to be angled downhill for the burr to cut wood. Inside bowls, it must also be used above the centerline so that if it catches, it is knocked into a void and not into the lower part of the bowl.

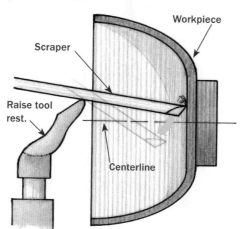

Scraper

Workpiece

Raise tool rest.

Centerline

On inside bowl work, the rest has to be raised so that you can slope and cant the scraper to the sweet angle slightly above the centerline, where it will be kicked safely into the air if it hits a hard spot. If you are below the centerline, the scraper will plow deeper into the wood, with nasty results.

Because the scraper removes so little wood, there is no need to grasp it as firmly as other turning tools. A scraper should be held like a captive bird—firmly enough that it can't fly away, but gently enough that you never ruffle a feather. Because of the pronounced downward angle necessary for the interiors of bowls, I often hold the handle in my right hand like a pencil with my left hand on the top of the shaft. This gives me a comfortable grip with a great feel for what is happening and control over the cutting action.

You also don't want the tool rest too close to the work, because the scraper needs room to move down in the event of a mishap. Although small scrapers often use the entire edge by design, large scrapers can overwhelm the turner if the entire edge is engaged. A

dome shape is very useful for bowl work, but the radius of the scraper should be less than the radius of the bowl or the entire edge will engage, with startling results.

One way to avoid catching the whole edge is to cant the scraper at an angle so that only a small part of it is cutting. Take care not to engage the elevated tip of the scraper against the bottom of the vessel or the scraper will be slammed flat on the rest, resulting in a nasty catch.

Add these scrapers next

Although you don't need to start with an arsenal of scrapers, after mastering the dome scraper, aim for the following collection, gradually adding custom-ground models.

A boat-tail scraper for flat surfaces

If you are tired of clouds of dust when trying to sand the surface of a platter flat, you need what I call a boat-tail scraper. It can also be used for fairing long, straight sections in spindle turning, such as tapered legs.

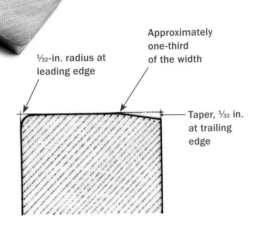

How to make a boat-tail scraper

Start with a square profile, round one corner, and relieve the other.

⅟₃₂-in. radius at leading edge

Approximately one-third of the width

Taper, ⅟₃₂ in. at trailing edge

Tool rest is your guide. Make sure the rest is an even distance from the workpiece, and run your knuckle against it to produce a flat surface.

Check your work. Use a straightedge to check if the surface is flat. If the rim interferes with using a rule, improvise with a piece of wood.

How to use a boat-tail scraper

The scraper is designed to cut from right to left, taking light cuts until the surface of the workpiece is flat. With care, it can also be used from left to right.

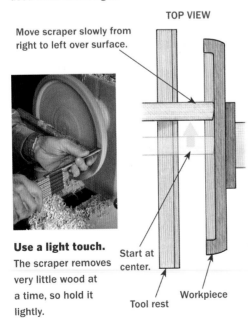

Move scraper slowly from right to left over surface.

TOP VIEW

Use a light touch. The scraper removes very little wood at a time, so hold it lightly.

Start at center.

Workpiece

Tool rest

Starting with a 1-in.- to 1½-in.-wide square-end scraper, grind a ⅟₃₂-in. radius at the left corner and taper the right-hand third of the tip by about ⅟₃₂ in. (see "How to make a boat-tail scraper," at left). The tool is designed to cut from right to left, but can also make very light cuts from left to right. The rounded corner allows the scraper to remove a good amount of material when cutting to the left, whereas the curved boat tail gets the trailing edge out of the way so it won't leave a line in the work.

As with the dome scraper, the heavier the boat-tail scraper, the better: If you are going to be in a head-on collision it is better to be in a very heavy vehicle. Likewise, a hard knot will affect a heavy scraper much less than a light one.

A V-scraper makes chucks, shoulders, and grooves

Take any ½-in.-wide scraper and grind a roughly 90-degree V-tip on it. Like all scrapers, the profile of the tip is ever-

Make a recess for a chuck

The V-scraper can be ground to match the jaws of a four-jaw chuck and then used to scrape a recess in the base of the workpiece.

Precise groove for a chuck. Hold the scraper against the chuck's jaw to check the angle required for the V-scraper. Then push the scraper into the workpiece until the recess fits the jaws on the chuck.

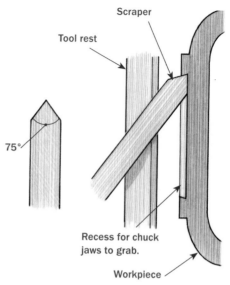

Scraper

Tool rest

75°

Recess for chuck jaws to grab.

Workpiece

Undercut a shoulder

The V-scraper can also be used to put a slight undercut on the shoulder of a turned pull, ensuring a gap-free fit with the drawer or door when it is installed.

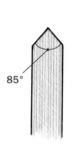

85°

Undercut shoulder. By grinding the V-scraper to less than 90 degrees, you can slightly undercut the shoulder of a pull for a better fit on the workpiece.

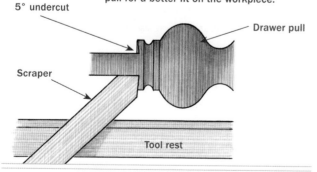

5° undercut

Scraper

Drawer pull

Tool rest

changing, based on the needs of the project or even the latest stage of the project.

Make custom scrapers for beads and coves

You also can use a variety of old tools as shopmade scrapers. These include old files, screwdrivers, and chisels. Generally used to cut beads or coves and known as form scrapers, these small scrapers are the epitome of perishable tooling: They are ground to a shape and reground to another to meet the needs of the job. Simply grind them to the desired shape, making sure that you don't overheat them if they are not made from high-speed steel (see the photos on p. 16).

If you use an old file, you can reduce the slight risk of it breaking by tempering the steel. Grind the area near the tip bright, and then place it in a household oven at 475°F. Watch carefully, and when the ground area turns bright blue (in about an hour), turn off the oven and allow the file to cool slowly. You can now grind and file a custom profile on the end.

Easiest way to form beads and coves. You can purchase scrapers designed to cut beads and coves, or you can custom-make your own from old screwdrivers and files.

Screwdriver scraper. Grind a round-nose profile on the tip of a screwdriver (left), and use it to scrape a small cove on spindle turnings such as these drawer pulls (right).

New use for an old file. After grinding away the teeth (above), temper the file in your oven. Now you can use another file to fine-tune the shape (left).

One plunge and done. The improvised scraper can create small beads far more quickly and easily than a spindle gouge.

Gouges

ERNIE CONOVER

I'll never forget King Heiple, the orthopedic surgeon who signed up for one of my turning classes a few years ago. When I called the class to gather 'round as I demonstrated a new technique, he was the student who was right by my side, carefully studying my every move. Then he would go over to his lathe and do what I did, except he did it better. Not many of us are blessed with the ability to master a new skill so quickly. But I have noticed that anyone who learns how to handle a gouge with aplomb will be far along the road to mastering turning itself.

Gouges can be divided into three categories: roughing-out, bowl, and spindle. When viewed in cross section, all are U-shaped, but their similarities end there.

Roughing-out gouges are the biggest of the bunch. They're used to make square stock round. Spindle gouges have the shallowest flutes. They're used for finely shaping the details on legs or posts. Bowl gouges have the deepest flutes and are employed when shaping vessels in faceplate turning.

Knowing a little about how gouges are made and what they're used for can help in deciding which types you need to add to your turning arsenal.

You'll need some tools and jigs to reshape and sharpen the gouges. Even premium tools leave the factory with a grind that's only a caricature of the proper shape. That problem

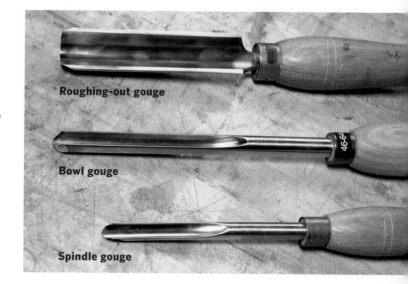

Roughing-out gouge

Bowl gouge

Spindle gouge

has plagued turners for more than a century. J. Lukin wrote of spindle gouges in his book, *The Lathe & Its Uses*, published in 1868: "When purchased, they require grinding, the bevel being too short. It is essential that this tool have a long bevel. It is impossible to do good work with the standard form of the tool which is, nevertheless, of frequent occurrence in the workshops of amateurs."

The best gouges are made of high-speed steel

Gouges were first manufactured by forging and many are still made that way. High-carbon steel is heated and hammered to the correct shape while hot. Premium gouges, made of high-speed steel, are machined into the proper shapes.

Roughing-out gouge

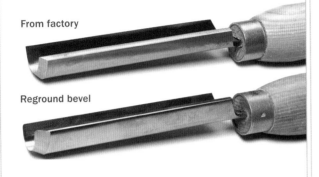

From factory

Reground bevel

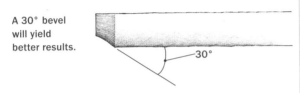

A 30° bevel
will yield
better results.

30°

A roughing-out gouge can remove large amounts of material quickly. It's used for rounding billets and cutting cylinders and tapers. One roughing-out gouge will serve most needs; I recommend getting one that's between ¾ in. and 1¼ in. wide. Most high-speed-steel roughing-out gouges come from the factory with square faces and medium bevels, about 45 degrees. The tool works much better with a longer bevel of about 30 degrees (see the drawing above).

To begin grinding, set up your jig. The Oneway sharpening jig, which I favor, has a V-shaped pocket welded to a square bar that slides into a mating piece attached below the grinder. The distance from the pocket to the wheel determines the bevel angle. As the pocket moves toward the grinder, the bevel length increases and the angle decreases.

Set the roughing-out gouge's handle in the pocket, lower the cutting edge against the grindstone, and roll the tool between your fingers for an even bevel (see the photo above). If you plan to use the roughing-out gouge to cut large coves, ease the edges of the corner bevels against the grindstone so that you won't catch the sharp edges against the workpiece.

Preparing spindle stock. A roughing-out gouge makes quick work of rounding a square billet.

Grinding a roughing-out gouge. The heel of a roughing-out gouge's handle rides in a Oneway sharpening jig's rest set for a 30-degree bevel. The author spins the tool between his fingers and applies even pressure against the grindstone.

High-carbon-steel tools

Only carbon is needed to make a good tool steel. But since the late 19th century, steelmakers have been adding other alloying ingredients, such as manganese, phosphorus, silicon, vanadium, and nickel, to their steels to make them tougher and more abrasion-resistant.

The heat-treating process is just as important as the basic steel. Soft steel is hardened and then tempered. When it arrives from the mill, steel is about Rc31 (Rockwell hardness scale). Most cutting tools need to be much harder if they are to hold an edge.

Heat-treating begins with hardening. The freshly forged tool is brought to cherry red and then quenched in water or oil. This leaves the steel at full hardness, about Rc64 for high-carbon tool steels. The steel is then tempered in a process called drawing.

High-speed-steel tools

In 1868, steelmakers came up with high-speed steel (HSS) by alloying tungsten (and later large amounts of molybdenum) into their steels. Because HSS does not forge well, these gouges are usually machined from round bar stock.

High-speed steel does hold an edge longer than high-carbon steel, but its real virtue is that the turner no longer has to worry about overheating the tool during grinding. Temperatures above 430°F begin to draw the temper of high-carbon tools, but HSS tools can be turned red hot, up to about 1,800°F, without loss of temper. That means you can use grinding wheels without a water bath. The cost of an HSS tool can be two to three times that of carbon steel, but it's well worth it.

Round is better

Most turners prefer a gouge made of round bar stock: The point of contact with the tool rest can be kept directly under the edge doing the cutting. Flatter tools have an oval-shaped bottom, and the contact point can be off to one side or the other, a less stable condition.

Combination gouges

Long HSS gouges whose flutes are deeper than those on spindle gouges but shallower than those on bowl gouges have recently been

Spindle gouge

The best spindle gouges are made of high-speed-steel round bar stock. They come from the factory with a very short bevel and a rather squarish profile at the tip, which makes it hard to get the point into tight quarters. I prefer to grind the sides into a fingernail profile with a rather long bevel. For spindle turning, the tool needs a long bevel of 25 degrees to 30 degrees. I also like a highly tapered profile, what I call a high-society fingernail shape, because the narrow point gets into tight places (see the drawing below). I know a good many turners, however, who do just fine with a rather blunt or workingman's fingernail. You may want to experiment to see what profile works best for the kind of work you do.

If you're just starting out, I recommend you buy two spindle gouges: ¼ in. and ½ in. diameter. For furniture-making purposes, these will usually suffice. Spindle gouges are sharpened using a pocket jig and a gooseneck clamp (see the top photo on p. 20). Adjust the jig for a 30-degree bevel angle, and swing the gouge from side to side across the grinding wheel. A jig allows you to get a consistent grind that would be difficult to do freehand without a lot of practice.

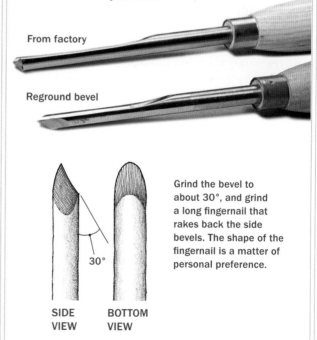

From factory

Reground bevel

Grind the bevel to about 30°, and grind a long fingernail that rakes back the side bevels. The shape of the fingernail is a matter of personal preference.

30°

SIDE VIEW   BOTTOM VIEW

introduced. The bevels on these gouges can be ground between 35 degrees and 45 degrees and will perform both faceplate or spindle work. However, these gouges do neither job as well as a dedicated gouge. Combination gouges cannot be ground to the really long bevel necessary for spindle work. Grinding a 30-degree side bevel creates a ragged burr on both sides of the fingernail where the metal has been ground too thin. If ground to a bowl-gouge contour, combination gouges lack sufficient flute depth to do a really good job. I find that they're best used for final cleanup on faceplate work.

Economy gouges

About 50 years ago, some large retailers began offering inexpensive lines of turning tools for hobbyists. These gouges have shorter and thinner blanks of steel and shorter handles. Such tools are still around. Their cross section is very flat—so flat that they don't do a good job of rolling beads or cutting deep coves. It's best to avoid them.

Tools for sharpening

Although I learned how to sharpen gouges by eye using a simple tool rest mounted on a bench grinder, I now prefer jigs for more accurate and consistent results.

Good jigs hold the tool at the proper angle when sharpening. Because lathe tools are round or oval-shaped, you need to rotate or swing them to shape the bevel correctly. Doing this freehand takes more skill than turning itself. I can recommend two brands of jigs: Oneway and Glaser. Both will help guide the tool around the grindstone with a greater sense of control than is possible with only a simple tool rest.

Not all grinding wheels are alike

I use an ordinary bench grinder with aluminum oxide wheels for most of my

Jigs simplify the task of sharpening. Using a Oneway sharpening jig and a gooseneck clamping fixture to hold the tool, the author swings a spindle gouge from side to side across the grinding wheel. Bevel angles are controlled by adjusting both the pocket jig's distance from the grinder and the angle on the gooseneck clamp.

Cutting coves and beads. Much of what's needed for furniture making can be performed with a spindle gouge.

grinding. New bench grinders usually come equipped with silicon carbide wheels, which are very hard and better suited for shaping garden tools.

When I do roughing work, I grind gouges on a 46-grit wheel. For finer cuts, I sharpen them on an 80-grit wheel. It's important to keep your grinding wheels trued and flat. For that, I use a diamond wheel dresser. If you will be grinding high-carbon-steel tools, you'll need to keep the tool cool during sharpening by regularly dipping it into a water bath to avoid drawing the temper. Bluing on high-speed steel won't affect the temper.

Finish by honing the edge

I always hone my spindle-turning tools after sharpening, but my bowl gouges usually get honed only when I'm ready to make final passes across a workpiece and want a really smooth surface.

For honing, I use a cushion-sewn buffing wheel impregnated with Dico® SRC stainless buffing compound, which is available at most hardware stores. To buff a gouge, hold it downhill against the wheel and touch up both the bevel and the back. Make sure the gouge is held tangentially to the wheel so that you don't round off the sharp cutting edge.

Bowl gouge

Traditional bowl gouges were forged with a deep U-shaped bevel, which was ground all the way around to 45 degrees. The cutting edge (what is called the face) of this tool is square to the shank.

Modern bowl gouges, machined from high-speed-steel round bar stock, generally have parabolic-shaped flutes. Factory grindings of this tool vary greatly among manufacturers, but many come with a 45-degree bevel ground all the way around. Most turners find the tool's performance can be improved by modifying this shape. Do this to the two primary bowl gouges you'll want to have in your tool kit: ½ in. and ¼ in. sizes.

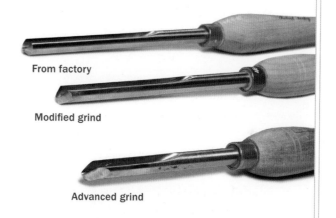

From factory

Modified grind

Advanced grind

MODIFIED GRIND

I favor an asymmetrical grind where the sides of the flute are raked back 15 degrees to 30 degrees and the nose bevel is reground to 60 degrees to 80 degrees. This allows you to cut cleanly across the axis of rotation without catching the corners of the tool or digging in too aggressively.

This grind works well when turning the inside of deep bowls because the nose bevel does not lose contact with the wood when it makes the sharp transition from the side wall to the bottom of the workpiece.

I use the Oneway sliding pocket jig with a matching gooseneck clamping fixture to sharpen bowl gouges. I slide the clamp 1¾ in. beyond the tip of the gouge, tighten the lock screw, and set the angle on the jig's arm. Different jigs have slightly different ways of adjusting bevel angles, so you'll need to refer to your manual. On the Oneway jig, the gouge is held in such a way that the gooseneck's arm pivots inside the pocket jig. You grind the gouge by swinging it from side to side, maintaining even pressure against the grindstone.

ADVANCED GRIND

Many bowl turners grind the side bevels back even more and increase the length of the lower bevel, too. If you want a longer bevel, bring the pocket in closer to the grinder. If you want more rake on the sides, adjust the gooseneck accordingly.

In skilled hands, a gouge with this grind will cut through reverse grain with nary any tearout, but it negates much of the forgiving nature of a modified-grind bowl gouge. Instead of rolling out of trouble, it tends to dig in deeper. Become proficient with one of the other grinds before progressing to this one.

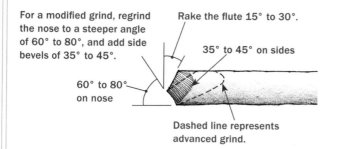

For a modified grind, regrind the nose to a steeper angle of 60° to 80°, and add side bevels of 35° to 45°.

Rake the flute 15° to 30°.

35° to 45° on sides

60° to 80° on nose

Dashed line represents advanced grind.

Mini Lathe
Model #: 70-100
Size: 12" x 16"
Size w/ Ext: 12" x
Speeds: 6 (430-3900 RPM)
1/2
Ser 090910005

Four-Jaw Chucks

RALPH TURSINI

Since their introduction to woodworkers in the mid-1980s, four-jaw chucks have been steadily replacing faceplates as the preferred way to turn hollow forms, because they make the process faster and easier, especially for beginning turners. But four-jaw chucks aren't just for bowls and vases. A chuck allows you to use a number of useful shopmade accessories for sanding, polishing, and turning small items. In fact, a four-jaw chuck is such a valuable tool that I advise my students to make it their next big purchase once they have a decent set of turning tools and some experience at the lathe.

Handles small parts . . .

Sands and polishes

A four-jaw chuck installs easily . . .

Grabs bowls tightly . . .

Choosing a chuck

When buying a chuck, it's important to consider not only the size of your lathe but also the size of the work you do.

A BIG CHUCK FOR BIG LATHES

Larger lathes (16-in. to 24-in. swing) are best matched to chucks with 4½-in. bodies. One downside: The bigger body gets in the way with small turnings, but a set of spigot jaws (see the sidebar on p. 28) solves the problem.

TWO OPTIONS FOR SMALLER LATHES

Mid-size and smaller lathes work best with 3½-in. chucks (middle). Another option for these lathes is a mini-chuck (right). Its 2½-in. body provides additional access near the chuck face.

Match the chuck to the lathe

Although there are exceptions, chucks come in two basic body sizes (4½ in. and 3½ in.) that correspond to the two basic classes of lathe (see "Choosing a chuck" above). You can put the smaller chuck on larger lathes with an adapter, but these can be difficult to remove and tend to amplify vibration, so I avoid them.

Because there are so many lathe models, chucks have a threaded insert that's specific to the lathe spindle, so you'll need to know the spindle diameter and thread pitch before you buy. If you have a modern lathe, knowing the manufacturer and model number will likely be enough, as most chuck manufacturers have an application chart to help you get the right insert.

Securing your work

You can use the chuck's jaws to grip a tenon or you can expand them into a recess, but it's best to grip the work because wood has greater compressive strength than tensile strength, especially perpendicular to the grain. This makes using a recess a delicate balance: Expand the jaws too much and your work will split; expand them too little and the workpiece could loosen. Rather than using a recess, it often makes sense to turn the work with a tenon (for gripping) that can be removed later.

The jaws that come with chucks have either a smooth, serrated, or dovetailed profile. I prefer the serrated profile, as it provides the best grip with the least amount of pressure. Dovetail jaws also hold well,

One wrench is easier than two. Chucks tightened with a pair of tommy bars (above left) cost less than chucks operated with a single wrench, but holding and tightening a workpiece can be a challenge. Chucks with a single wrench (above right) allow you to hold the workpiece with one hand and tighten the jaws with the other.

Better to grip than expand. Chuck jaws can either grip a tenon (right) or expand into a recess (bottom right), but it's best to grip a tenon whenever possible because wood has more compressive strength than tensile strength. The owner's manual is the best place to look for information on shaping a tenon or recess that matches an individual chuck's jaw profile. Accessory jaws will have different requirements than standard jaws.

How jaws work

Tenons need a square or slightly undercut shoulder for solid seating.

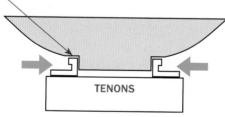

TENONS

Some jaws require an angled recess.

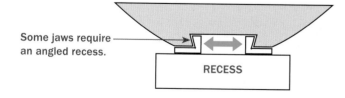

RECESS

Match the tenon to the jaws. Even though most chucks can grip through a 2-in.-dia. range, there is a sweet spot where they make full contact with the workpiece (left). Outside the sweet spot, the grip is compromised (below).

Jaws in full contact with tenon

Limited contact area

especially inside a recess, but matching a tenon to their exact shape can be tedious.

Jaw sizes and profiles

The most versatile jaws grip tenons that are roughly one-half to three-quarters of the chuck's body diameter. Not surprisingly, this is the set that is generally included with the chuck body. Accessory jaws will vary with the kinds of turnings you're doing. For instance, spigot jaws are great for holding small parts (down to about ⅜ in. diameter) like knobs and pulls. If you want to make vases and other longer hollow forms, deeper jaws like Oneway's Tower Jaws will get a very firm grip on a long tenon (see "Accessory jaws worth having" on p. 28).

Must-have accessories

You'll find both a screw center and a chuck spur center invaluable for initial shaping of the blank and preparing a tenon that can be clamped inside the chuck jaws (see photos on the facing page). Most chucks come with a screw center, which is the fastest way to mount a blank for initial profiling and for shaping the tenon. Screw centers hold better

in face grain than in end grain, and they are not all equal. I've found that the screw centers made by Oneway and Vicmarc hold the best.

Unlike a screw center, which requires a flat face on the blank, spur centers can be used with burls and other irregular-shaped blanks. Chuck-mounted versions save time and handling because you don't have to remove the chuck to use them. Despite their utility, chuck spurs aren't included with most chucks. You'll have to buy one. My favorite is from Oneway.

In my experience, when it comes to purchasing, chucks are definitely one of those items where you get what you pay for. High-quality chucks have precise machining for smooth operation and a good grip. Conversely, I've had blanks loosen on low-priced chucks even when I thought I had really cranked them down.

Turning a bowl is easier with a 4-jaw chuck. Relatively uniform blanks with a flat side can be rough-profiled with a screw center. The blank should make even contact with the chuck jaws to minimize vibration. Screw centers usually come with the chuck.

Irregular blanks. Burls and other irregular-shaped blanks require a chuck spur center and the tailstock for initial profiling. A ⅜-in.-deep hole the same diameter as the spur prevents the blank from sliding as it's secured to the lathe.

Shape the outside of the bowl and turn a tenon. With the outside of the blank roughed out, turn a tenon that fits the chuck. The finished tenon should have straight sides and a square shoulder for the best grip.

TWO WAYS TO MOUNT THE BLANK

Spur center

Screw center

Flip and hollow. Clamp the bowl's tenon in the chuck, making sure it is fully seated (above). With the bowl secured, hollow the interior (right). Keeping the sides and bottom a uniform thickness makes cracks less likely.

Accessory jaws worth having

You can easily swap the standard jaws with accessory jaws. Spigot jaws are great for turning small projects like pulls and ornaments. Adding deep jaws gives the chuck a firm grip on larger vases and boxes.

Spigot jaws offer a tight radius for small work. The long jaws also provide clearance from the chuck for turning and sanding small parts.

Deep jaws provide a better grip for large and long vessels.

Reverse it. To finish the foot, you have to flip the bowl one last time. Tursini slips it over a chucked mandrel (right), protecting the bowl with a piece of "fun foam." Then he moves the tailstock into place (below).

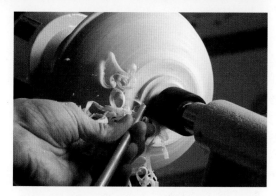

Finish the foot. Using a gouge, turn away most of the tenon and form the bowl's foot.

Break off the nub. The goal is to leave only a small button of stock.

Why a chuck beats a faceplate

Faceplates are the traditional way to turn hollow forms and they're still a viable method—especially for extremely heavy blanks. But they have a few drawbacks.

Working around the plate is cumbersome. Even the smallest faceplate will hamper access to the stock surrounding it.

Faceplates leave deep screw holes. Over-zealous hollowing can expose the screws that mount the blank to the faceplate, ruining the turning.

Trim with a chisel. Use a chisel to pare any remaining stock flush with the bowl's bottom.

Sharpening Gouges

MIKE MAHONEY

In my years of teaching wood turning, I've noticed that many students have trouble learning how to grind gouges correctly. That's understandable. Unlike most other turning tools, a bowl or spindle gouge must be moved in two directions simultaneously—rolled against the grinding wheel while being swept from side to side. That's the only good way to keep the gouge's distinctive fingernail profile and a cutting edge beveled at a consistent angle along the curved end of the tool.

The proper bevel is crucial for cutting wood efficiently. As a rule, the more acute the bevel, the cleaner the gouge will cut and the less force you'll have to use. For most turnings, a 50-degree bevel is better than one of 70 degrees, and 40 degrees is better still.

The sharpening jigs I've seen produce an uneven bevel, invariably 16-degrees to 20-degrees more acute on the sides than at the tip. That's because they aren't designed to swing the gouge from side to side. As a result, the gouge will vibrate when used and will dull quickly.

I believe it's better to grind gouges freehand. The technique described here, which I adopted after watching my friend and master turner Stuart Batty, is simple, effective, and easy to learn.

What a keen edge does. A properly sharpened gouge cuts efficiently and doesn't need a lot of muscle to do its work.

Make a template. Cut one corner of a piece of scrap at a 40-degree angle and use it to mark the grinder platform.

Angle the grinder platform. Use trial and error to set the platform at a 40-degree angle (or close to it), which will be the bevel angle on the gouge.

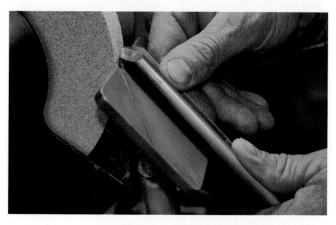

Grind the nose to check the angle. Test the platform angle by lightly grinding the nose of the gouge, then checking the result with a protractor or angle gauge.

Set your grinder for the proper angles

Handbooks and experts give different recommendations for optimum bevel angles, but Batty and I have found through experience that spindle and bowl gouges work best with a bevel of about 40 degrees. As it happens, that magic number represents the bevel angle, the amount of side-to-side movement you make when grinding, and the amount of bevel on the top side. Here's how to set up your grinder to get a consistent 40-degree bevel.

First, mark guidelines on the grinder platform 40 degrees left and right of the center of the grinding surface. They will help you get a consistent side-to-side sweep. Make a template from scrapwood cut to the same size as the platform. Mark the guidelines with an indelible marker.

Next, adjust the angle of the platform. Set it by eye to an angle that looks close to 40 degrees, then test it by grinding the bevel on the nose of the gouge. Check the result with an angle gauge or protractor, and tweak the platform angle as needed. Don't worry if the angle isn't exact; a couple of degrees either side of 40 won't matter. Once you have the platform at the correct angle, grind the bevel on the nose again and recheck it.

Grind a fresh cutting surface

The next stage of grinding deliberately flattens the cutting edge so you will have a fresh surface to grind back to. Hold the tool in line with the grinding wheel with the flute face down on the platform (see the top left photos on p. 32). Lift the gouge from the platform slightly as you pass it over the wheel a couple of times; that will create a slight convex surface overall. If you hold the gouge against the platform the whole time, the wheel will leave a concave surface, which gives the gouge a tendency to catch in the work.

Start a new cutting edge. With the gouge's flute facing down, grind away the cutting edge. The resulting thin face creates a guide for the last stage of sharpening.

To sharpen the edge, roll and swing

Begin with the gouge in line with the grinding wheel and the flute facing up (see the drawing at right). Keep the gouge flat on the grinder platform, holding it by the metal just above the ferrule to keep the grinding angle consistent. If you hold the tool by the handle, you may be inclined to lift it off the platform, thus changing the angle.

Roll the gouge counterclockwise while moving it to the left. You want to end with the flute facing to the left and the gouge lined up with your 40-degree line on the left side of the grinder platform. As you bring the gouge up to the line, be careful not to roll it too far; if you do, you'll make the end of the bevel convex.

Repeat the maneuver, rolling the gouge clockwise while moving it toward the other 40-degree mark.

Grind the bevel

To sharpen the edge, start with the gouge centered on the grinder platform in line with the grinding wheel. Roll the gouge while simultaneously swinging it to the side to the 40-degree mark on the grinder platform. Keep the gouge flat on the grinder platform to maintain a consistent grinding angle. Sharpen one side at a time. Finish by blending in the bevel.

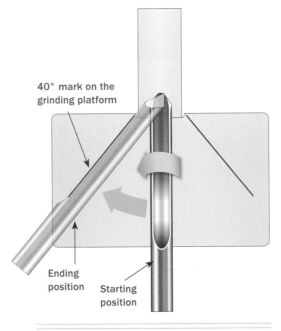

40° mark on the grinding platform

Ending position

Starting position

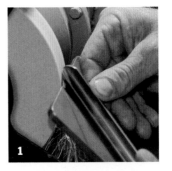

Start with the flute facing up and the tool centered on the grinder platform. Sweep the gouge in an arc to the left, simultaneously rolling the tool so that the gouge faces left. End at the 40-degree guideline on the grinder platform. Then sweep and roll the gouge to the right.

Turning Furniture Parts

PETER GALBERT

I had almost no idea how to use a lathe when I built my first Windsor chair 13 years ago, even though I'd built plenty of furniture by then. So I set about teaching myself to turn by digging through books and magazines for more information. As a woodworker new to turning, I discovered pretty quickly there's a lot they don't tell you.

There is a learning curve in jumping from curious furniture maker to competent turner.

I'll show you how to get through it quickly as you turn a basic cylinder, the starting point for any spindle, and then add some tapers and tenons. Along the way, I'll share the tips I wish I'd known when I started turning, particularly things like how to hold the tool and move your body for clean cuts.

Luckily, getting started isn't expensive. Furniture makers turn mostly spindles (workpieces secured at both ends on a lathe),

Mount the blank. Find the center by drawing corner-to-corner lines on both ends, then use the marks to line up the workpiece on the lathe's centers. Punch the intersection with an awl.

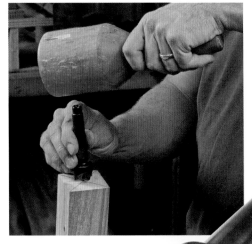

Tap the drive center. To mount a spur center, remove it from the lathe and pound it into the end of the workpiece to create a pattern of indents.

Line it up. The awl and spur marks will register the piece when you seat it between the drive and tail centers. Line everything up and then tighten the tailstock to secure the blank.

Keep it close. Move the tool rest about ⅛ in. away from the workpiece, and keep it at about the height of the centerline.

TIP Tools will glide more easily over a smooth, straight tool rest, so file it smooth and polish it with diamond plates or sharpening stones. Then coat it with wax.

which doesn't require an especially powerful machine, although a longer one is better. And you can cut almost any shape with a ¾-in. roughing gouge, a ⅛-in. diamond parting tool, a ⅜-in. detail gouge, and a ¾-in. oval skew chisel. Buy those four tools instead of a whole "kit" and you'll save a pretty penny. You can spend that savings on a few essential accessories I'll recommend later.

Start from square one

Whether you're making table legs or drawer pulls, every turned piece starts as a blank.

Begin with a square one at least ⅛ in. wider than the widest diameter of the finished spindle. That should leave room for roughing and shaping.

It's important to get the blank centered properly on the lathe, because if it's off on one end you'll remove a lot of extra material to get an even cylinder. So draw corner-to-corner lines on both ends, punch the two intersections with an awl, and use the indent to line up the lathe's drive center and tail center (see the photos on the facing page).

If you're using a traditional spur center, remove it from the lathe and hammer it into the end of the blank before mounting the whole piece back in the lathe. Use the spur marks to line up the workpiece. If you don't have a center yet, I recommend you buy a steb center instead. A steb center has a circle of teeth with a spring loaded-pin in the middle, and acts like a clutch if a spinning piece catches a gouge. It's a more forgiving design, especially for beginners, and it's easier to mount because it stays in the lathe. Just line up the pin by eye. It's a spring, so you can always loosen the tail and move it if need be. With either type of center, tighten the tailstock enough that the piece won't spin freely by hand. Don't overtighten or you can damage the lathe's bearings.

Now set the tool rest about ⅛ in. from the widest part of the blank, about even with the center. Rotate the blank by hand to make sure it will clear the tool rest as it spins. Keep the rest in the same relative position as you rough out the blank and the diameter shrinks.

Basic roughing technique

A perfect cylinder actually starts as a series of gentle, overlapping tapers that eventually get evened out. That initial taper ensures you're always cutting downhill later on when you smooth the surface. Downhill cuts mean you won't run the risk of catching the gouge on an exposed bit of end grain, which can pop out a wood chunk and or send the tool skittering. For both initial tapering and subsequent straightening, use the roughing gouge.

The basic strategy is simple. A right-handed turner would start cutting at the headstock end, always working from right to left to break the edges and rough out the subtle taper. Start the first pass about 3 in. from the headstock and cut back toward the headstock. Start each subsequent pass about that same distance farther away. Once you reach the end of the tool rest, or the spindle, keep cutting lightly along the full length of the section until the edges have all broken and the piece has begun to turn round. Then slide the tool rest down the lathe's bed and repeat the process until the whole spindle tapers roughly from end to end. There may be bumps, particularly where you've moved the tool rest, but don't worry, you'll smooth them away afterward.

At this stage of bringing the piece from square to round, there are a couple of important points to keep in mind. First, move with your legs (see the bottom photos on p. 36). Your body position and stance are difference-makers when it comes to clean

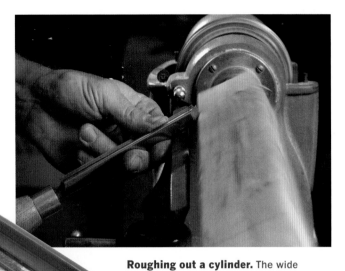

Roughing out a cylinder. The wide bevel and deep flute make this tool easy to control while hogging out material from a blank.

¾-in. roughing gouge

Drop the tool into the cut. Let the bevel ride high on the blank before entering the cut. Draw the gouge back slowly and angle it down to drop the cutting edge into the workpiece.

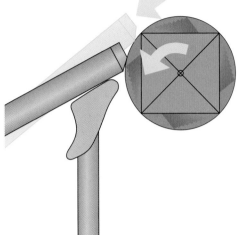

cuts. New turners make the mistake of moving the gouge by pushing their arms or rotating their waist. Those movements make the tool travel in an arc, and leave the turner constantly trying to compensate to cut evenly. Instead, keep your arms and upper body fixed in the same position and generate side-to-side movement from your legs and hips, pivoting your weight from one foot to the other. This keeps the gouge straight throughout the cut. This is easier to do if you align your body so that it feels comfortable at the end of the cut, rather than the beginning. Face the lathe in front of where your cut will end. Then pivot your weight to your right foot to start the cut. As you move through the cut, pivot your weight back to your left foot.

Also, never stab the gouge straight into a workpiece or it will scrape the wood instead

Move with the legs and hips. Galbert starts a cut with his arms, waist, and torso locked in position and his weight on his right foot (right). This ensures even cuts because he can hold the gouge in the same position and move by shifting his weight to his other foot (far right).

Maintain a skew cut

Skewing the gouge stabilizes the bevel against the already-cut section, leaving a cleaner surface and an easier-to-control tool.

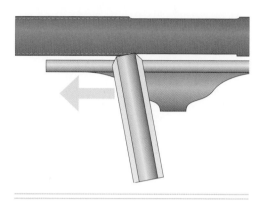

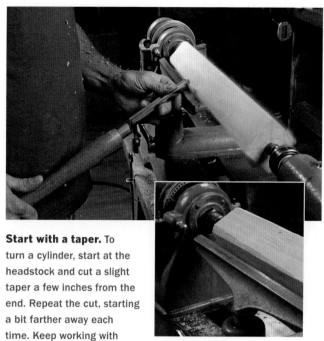

Start with a taper. To turn a cylinder, start at the headstock and cut a slight taper a few inches from the end. Repeat the cut, starting a bit farther away each time. Keep working with overlapping passes to create a rough taper along the blank (inset photo). Keep working toward the headstock to bring the taper closer to a straight cylinder (below) before moving the tool rest to the next section. When you are done, the whole blank will have a slight taper.

of cutting it. Scraping leaves a poor surface and creates lots of dust and the potential for serious tearout. Instead, ride the bevel up high on the spinning piece without cutting, and slowly draw it back, lifting the bottom of the handle to drop the edge and engage the workpiece. Exit the cut the same way,

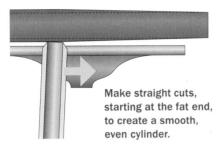

Make straight cuts, starting at the fat end, to create a smooth, even cylinder.

Finish with a cylinder. After carrying the taper to the tailstock end, Galbert starts there with a series of straight, shallow cuts to turn the long taper into a cylinder and smooth away any high spots.

by riding the bevel back up. Always skew the gouge, too. That way, the bevel rides on the just-cut surface, which will support the cutting edge ahead of it as you move. This, too, makes for cleaner, safer cuts.

Last, throughout the whole motion, don't hold the gouge too tightly. A heavy grip limits the range of movement and makes it hard to feel the feedback from a spinning workpiece. Grip it like a bird, just tight enough to keep it from flying away.

Using a parting tool. Point the tool straight at the blank with the bevel riding it. Draw the edge back and down to enter the cut.

As the diameter shrinks, you'll need to keep the edge moving down and toward the center.

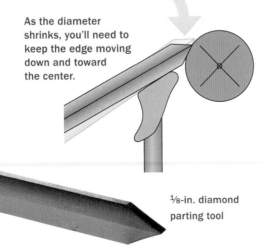

⅛-in. diamond parting tool

Set your landmarks. Galbert starts taper cuts by first sizing the diameters at the beginning and end. Set a caliper for the desired diameter and slide it into the parting-tool cut.

Other landmarks. This turning will get tapered at both ends, with a flattish section between. Shallow parting-tool marks define the thick ends of the taper.

Even the cylinder

Finish straightening the taper and evening out the cylinder by taking a series of straight passes with the gouge. Start at the tailstock end and drop the bevel in so that you're taking a very light cut. This time, run the gouge straight along the tapered piece. The cutting edge will take increasingly thinner shavings until at some point the gouge's

Start cutting at the end. Make a series of ever-widening passes to work down to your narrowest diameter without going deeper than your high point at the fat end of the taper. The taper will be a bit rough, but Galbert will smooth it with a skew chisel.

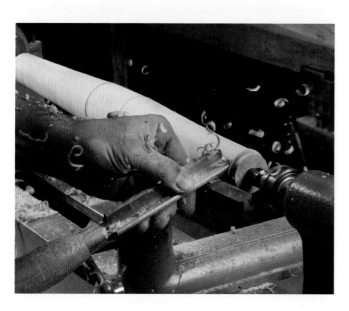

Switch directions on double tapers. To do the other taper, work toward the tailstock, moving left to right. Remember to skew the gouge into the cut.

edge will naturally come out of the cut as it moves along. Keep cutting with thin, straight passes to even out the taper, trim any high spots, and leave a uniform shape. Check the diameter of the cylinder with a caliper to make sure it's thin enough. If not, keep taking long, thin passes to remove material evenly and to leave a smooth surface for cutting shapes.

Tapers and cigars

You can turn your uniform cylinder into two elegant furniture parts, complete with precise tenons on the ends. The easiest shape is a simple taper. Create it by sizing the beginning and end of the taper with the parting tool, checking with a caliper set to the desired dimension.

Don't stab the parting tool straight into the workpiece. Enter a cut with the bevel riding on the round, and draw the tool back slowly to engage the tip. Exit the cut the same way. It helps to wiggle the parting tool side-to-side just a bit to widen the kerf while cutting. It also makes it easier to check your progress with a caliper as the work spins.

For measuring diameter, I prefer my Galbert Caliper (available from www.petergalbertchairmaker.com) because it won't catch the kerf's edges and reads dimensions directly without any setup.

Use a roughing gouge to remove the waste between the two parting-tool cuts, but don't cut down to the very bottom of the kerf. Leave just a little bit of material that you can remove during final smoothing with a skew chisel.

For a basic cigar shape, like those on turned Shaker legs or Windsor-chair stretchers, cut slightly rounded tapers on both ends of the cylinder the exact same way.

You can use the same technique to form accurate tenons. Just size the shoulder and ends and then gouge out the waste. Check that the diameter is even along the tenon using an open-ended wrench. Its wider surface makes it easier to see high and low spots.

Turning a tenon: Size the shoulder and ends first. Cut tenons like tapers, but with the same diameter at both ends. The parting tool works better if used slightly away from the end, supported on both sides of the cut.

Scoop out the middle. Remove the waste at the end, and then take straight, even cuts with a roughing gouge (left). The thick jaws of a wrench (right) make it easy to find high spots, whether the piece is spinning or not.

Learn to Turn Spindles

ERNIE CONOVER

In many ways turning is the simplest branch of woodworking: All turning is a bead, a cove, a cylinder, or a taper; if you can cut these four shapes, you can turn anything. Likewise, there is no need to begin with a rack full of tools: a roughing-out gouge, a spindle gouge, a V-parting tool, and a skew chisel are sufficient for the novice.

Why is it, then, that the early enthusiasm of many beginners turns to frustration in the face of sustained difficulties? The answer can be summed up in two words—tool preparation. Few tools come from the factory with the correct grind, and none will be as sharp as it could be. I'll demonstrate how to put a correct grind on all of them and how to keep them sharp; then and only then can you start to make shavings.

Selecting and preparing your tools

I urge you to avoid sets of tools. They may or may not contain a good spindle gouge, they will likely have a skew chisel that is too narrow, and there will be too many scrapers. Buy high-speed-steel tools, which are only slightly more expensive than regular (high-carbon) steel tools and hold an edge longer; you cannot draw the temper during grinding, even if you overheat the tool.

Roughing-out gouge

I recommend a 1¼-in. gouge, but the ¾-in. version is a good, less-costly second choice.

The roughing-out gouge can be ground with a blunt fingernail face, but I prefer it with a square face because it is easier to cut up to a shoulder. The tool can be ground either with the handle resting in a pocket holder (see the top photo on p. 43) or simply braced against your thigh.

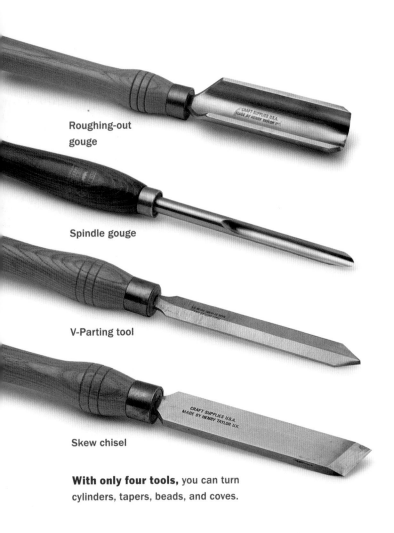

Roughing-out gouge

Spindle gouge

V-Parting tool

Skew chisel

With only four tools, you can turn cylinders, tapers, beads, and coves.

Spindle gouge

A ½-in. spindle gouge will be your work-horse, so invest wisely. Check the shaft to make sure the steel is from a round bar rather than from a thin section of rolled steel. A spindle gouge operates best with a long fingernail grind but is usually delivered with a short blunt grind (see the bottom left photo on the facing page). Although it is possible to grind a fingernail by eye on a bench grinder, it is difficult to do. Oneway, Sorby, and Tormek® all make jigs to simplify this task. You can also find a shop-built jig on p. 97 of *The Lathe Book* (The Taunton Press, 2001) and at www.finewoodworking.com.

I tend to grind a very long fingernail, which I call a high-society grind, but other turners work successfully with a somewhat more blunt fingernail. Experiment to find what length suits your turning style, but always polish your fingernail to a razor-sharp edge. This can be done with slipstones, but with a buffing wheel it's far quicker and you are less likely to miss a section.

V-parting tool

Also called a cutoff tool, the V-parting tool is used for cutting off work in the lathe. It is also used with calipers to establish sizes for duplicate parts, to create shoulders next to a bead, and to make tenons. The tool works fine with a hollow grind, and the best cross section is the diamond shape, which has much less friction during a cut than cheaper, square cross-section tools. I suggest getting either a ¹⁄₁₆-in. or ⅛-in. tool.

Skew chisel

The edge of this tool, in addition to being double beveled, is also skewed about 25 degrees to 30 degrees to its axis. The skew chisel is the one tool that should not be hollow-ground; it works much better with a flat (or even slightly convex) bevel. Luckily, all skews seem to be delivered with a flat bevel and can be honed on whetstones. If, however, your skew collides with a chuck or lands point-first on concrete, you will have to regrind it. The fastest way to do this and keep it flat is on the side of the wheel, which most grinding manuals advise against. I do it, but I use light pressure on a 1-in.-thick wheel. If you have a Tormek or other super-slow-speed wet grinder, you can use the side of this wheel with complete safety.

A skew slides more easily on the rest if you break the sharp edges of the shank. Touch the four corners of the shank to a grinder, then buff or stone them. The width of a 1-in. chisel allows much more time to judge when things are going awry and to make corrections before disaster strikes.

Preparing the tools for use

Blunt factory grind

Fingernail grind

Roughing-out gouge. Rest the handle in a pocket holder and rotate the tool against the grinding wheel.

A nautical comparison. To reshape the blunt profile of a factory-ground spindle gouge, use a special jig mounted in the pocket holder. The fingernail profile will resemble the bow of a cruise ship.

A V-parting tool works best with a hollow grind. To create the grind, use either a 6-in. or 8-in. wheel.

When necessary, regrind a skew chisel. Though it's not recommended in the manual, you can use the side of a 1-in.-thick wheel. Apply gentle pressure and wear eye protection.

Mastering the basics of spindle turning

Now that the tools have been sorted out, it is time to start turning. The best way to practice is to cut a dozen hardwood billets 2 in. square by 8 in. long. Find the exact centers of the first billet using a center finder, and make a small indentation using a hole punch or a blunt nail. This aids alignment with the headstock and the tailstock centers. Set the tool rest about two-thirds of the way up the blank just above the centerline of the lathe. Make sure the blank can turn freely.

Master the cylinder

Mount a square blank between centers and position the tool rest just above the centerline of the lathe. Raise the handle of the roughing-out gouge until the heel clicks on the blank.

Rounding the billet. Take light passes with the roughing-out gouge to gradually turn the blank round.

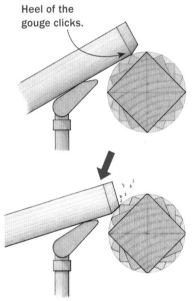

Heel of the gouge clicks.

Lower the gouge's cutting edge until it just starts to cut.

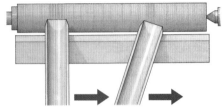

For fast rough cuts, move the gouge laterally. Maintain the same cutting angle and keep the tool 90 degrees to the blank.

For smooth cuts, angle the roughing-out gouge in the direction of the cut and move slowly.

Turning a cylinder

To make a billet round, use a roughing-out gouge. Present the gouge high (the handle low) so that just the heel of the bevel touches the work and clicks. Your right hand should be on the forward part of the handle with your thumb and forefinger on the ferrule. (Holding farther back on the handle gives you less feel for the bevel on the work.) Lower the cutting edge by raising the handle until the gouge just starts to cut. Ride the bevel in a shear cut, moving the tool laterally. Maintain the angle you have established until the work just starts to become round.

Turning a taper

The traditional tool for cutting a taper is the skew (see the photos on the facing page). Place the corner of the tool on the rest and present the tool high (handle low) and as

square as possible to the work. Now raise the handle until the bevel rubs in a shear cut. The cut should take place over no more than half the length of the cutting edge but biased toward the heel. Once the cut has been established, slide the tool laterally, maintaining the same angle to the work. Move it with the heel leading and the toe following behind the cut. To cut in the opposite direction, turn the tool over.

The roughing-out gouge and the spindle gouge can also cut tapers. Angling the gouge slightly in the direction you wish to cut will make it easy to produce cylinders and gentle tapers.

Cutting coves

The only way to cut a cove is with a spindle gouge (see p. 46). Start by drawing a series of pencil lines ½ in. apart on a freshly turned cyl-

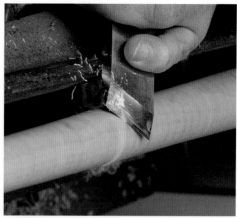

Cutting tapers. To cut a smooth and gentle taper, angle the roughing-out gouge in the direction you are cutting (left) and increase the pressure slightly. Use the skew in the same manner (above).

inder. Use only the very tip of the gouge during the entire process and keep the bevel parallel to the surface. Think of it as if you were mowing a ditch. If you mow along the ditch, the mower is level, but the mower increasingly leans as you move up the sides. Your gouge should roll in the same way, but think of the bevel and not the flute (shank) of the gouge as the mower. The bevel should always be perpendicular to the grain as you cut.

Your grip on the spindle gouge should be relaxed, and your hand placement should be the same as with the roughing-out gouge. Most beginners try to lock the handle against their hip; however, this holding method results in more catches because the user is trying to overpower the physics of the lathe rather than letting the machine and the tool cut as they are designed to. You cannot overcome physics—at least not for very long.

Present the tool high with the heel of the bevel rubbing and the tool square to the axis of the spindle. Lower the cutting edge by raising the handle until you cut a very small

depression at the exact center of one of your ½-in. layouts.

To cut the right-hand side of the cove, roll the gouge so that the top of the flute moves from the 12 o'clock position to approximately 11 o'clock. Touch down the tip of the gouge just beyond where the right-hand side of the cove begins and sweep down to the bottom of the cove, rolling the flute back to the 12 o'clock position. This roll has to be controlled and uniform, and the handle must have room to move, so don't lock it against your hip.

Now repeat the process to cut the left-hand side of the cove, rolling the flute to about 1 o'clock and touching down just beyond the left-hand side. At the bottom of the cove, the tool will have to slide very slightly forward on the rest to get to the bottom of the cove and still have the bevel rubbing because it is a farther reach to the smaller diameter. Now go to the other side of the cove and repeat a mirror image of what you have just done, alternating between left and right but always ending up at the exact center.

You cannot cut a cove that is a lot narrower than your gouge. Smaller coves get a narrower gouge. The process is much like chopping a log in two with an ax. The cut has to be wider than the ax. You need to cut from each edge to the exact center, cutting downhill on the grain. Cutting the wrong way will likely result in a fuzzy cut or a catch. Think of it as stroking a furry animal.

Cutting beads

The opposite of a cove is a bead, and in my opinion cutting a bead is a more difficult task to master. It is my very strong opinion that the only way to turn beads consistently is to use a spindle gouge. Using the skew for this task has its partisans, but for the small beads normally encountered in spindle turning, it is a risky business.

A good-looking bead (at least in most furniture turning) is not a half circle but rather an ellipse. Therefore, it is not as high as it is wide. To get ready for this exercise, use the V-parting tool to make ⅛-in. cuts into a cylinder; space the cuts ⅜ in. apart. This will yield a row of ⅜-in.-wide ridges that are called roundels.

Use a spindle gouge to cut coves

Once you have turned a few 8-in. blanks to cylinders, mark them with a series of lines ½ in. apart. Then start cutting coves.

Stay in touch. Keep your left hand near the tip of the tool, and always keep the tool in contact with the tool rest.

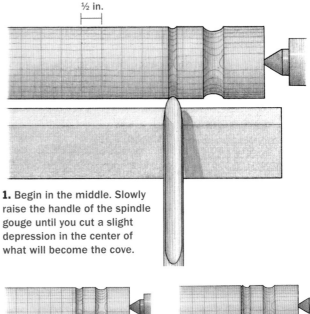

½ in.

1. Begin in the middle. Slowly raise the handle of the spindle gouge until you cut a slight depression in the center of what will become the cove.

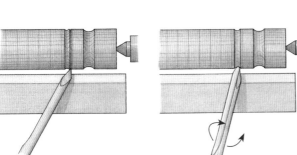

2. Next, cut at the top of the right-hand side of the cove and work downward.

3. Sweep the handle back toward the tailstock while rotating the tool clockwise.

4. Keep sweeping until the flute is at 12 o'clock at the bottom of the arc.

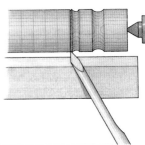

5. Repeat the cutting process starting from the other side and moving the handle to the left.

Cutting a cove is like chopping a log with an ax. Gradually deepen the cut, working alternately from both sides.

Like the cove, the bead is cut in two stages, one half at a time and always downhill. To cut the right-hand side of the bead, start at the center of the roundel with the gouge angled slightly to the right. This allows you to pick up the major diameter of the roundel without cutting into it. Cut to the right while sweeping the handle around to the left until you are cutting toward the tailstock. This also requires rolling the flute from a little past 12 o'clock until nearly 2 o'clock, sliding the tool slightly backward on the tool rest and raising the handle to keep cutting on the very point. At this point you will be about halfway to the base of the bead.

To cut the elliptical shape of the bead, you must move the handle to the right. Once you reach the base of the bead, the bevel of the gouge should be almost perpendicular to the main axis of the workpiece, with the flute facing 3 o'clock. If you were to continue pushing (very hard), you would cut right through the center of the billet. Simply

Use a spindle gouge to cut consistent beads

Before you can cut a bead, first remove the waste in every alternate section to leave a series of ridges, called roundels.

Cutting a bead. A good-looking bead is elliptical, not a half circle. Remove the wood in a series of light cuts.

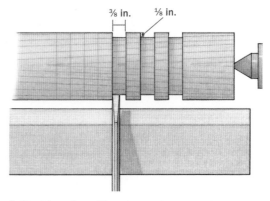

1. Start by using a V-parting tool to make ⅛-in.-deep cuts ⅜ in. apart. This will leave a series of raised ridges, or roundels.

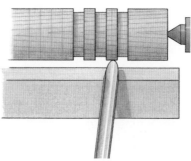

2. Next, place the gouge just to the right of the center, with the tip of the tool angled slightly to the right.

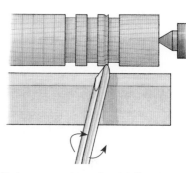

3. As you cut down the right-hand side, move the handle to the right and roll the tool clockwise, keeping the bevel perpendicular to the grain.

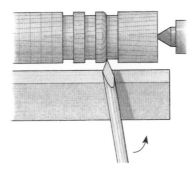

4. When you reach the base of the bead, the bevel of the gouge will be nearly 90 degrees to the cylinder, and the tool handle will be to your right.

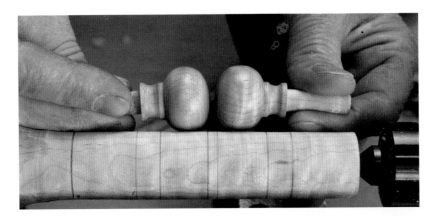

Now turn some drawer pulls. The skills learned while turning beads and coves can be put to good use by turning drawer pulls. Turn a pair of drawer pulls from the same blank. It not only saves time but also yields a matching pair of pulls.

The tenon is cut first. Make a series of cuts with the V-parting tool using a wrench as a guide.

Cut a small cove. Center the spindle gouge and gradually raise the handle to increase the depth.

Worry-free beads. With the depth of the bead already defined on both sides by the V-parting tool, round over the sides of the bead with a series of light cuts.

Don't be ashamed to sand your work. Particularly with curly wood, some tearout is inevitable and is easily removed by sanding.

trying to push the gouge forward once you reach the halfway point will result in a 45-degree flank to the bead.

Now repeat a mirror image of what you have just done to the left. It is quite normal for the beginner to cut asymmetrical beads, as we all have a bit of left-right bias. Practice will cure this problem. On larger beads you have to start closer to the edge of the roundel

and just round the corner on the first pass. Successive passes enhance the shape. Don't try to take too much material with one pass.

The visual impact of a bead is greatly enhanced by inscribing the edges with the toe of a skew. I think this sets apart the bead from the surrounding, your mind completing the shape of the bead inside the turning on a subliminal level.

Duplicate Spindles by Hand

KIM CARLETON GRAVES

If you're a furniture maker, duplicating parts on a lathe is as fundamental a skill as duplicating parts on a tablesaw. Hobbyists and small custom shops usually have only a few spindles to duplicate: four legs for a table, 16 front legs for a set of eight chairs. You are much better off doing this work by hand rather than on a mechanical duplicator. The results are superior because edges are crisper and shapes are better defined. Also, for small runs, handwork is almost always faster.

To demonstrate standard hand duplication, I've chosen a stool leg designed by my friend and client, Anatoli Lapushner, owner of Anatoli's Restoration in New York City. This design has four elements—the pommel, the large swell, the taper, and the foot—that make it particularly challenging (see the left photo on p. 51).

Duplicate parts don't have to be identical. More precisely, only some dimensions must be identical. In this example, only the length of the leg and the placement of the mortises are critical. The turning can be less accurate. The human eye wants to see symmetries. If the major diameters and the vertical placement of elements are relatively close, no one will notice if you're off by ⅟₁₆ in. dia. or even ⅛ in. dia. Identical parts have a dead, cookie-cutter look.

Duplicating spindles is a simple procedure: Make a pattern, mill the blanks, transfer the pattern to the blanks, and turn the work.

Make the pattern first

A full-size pattern can be used to copy an existing spindle or to create an original one. Simply set, check, and reset calipers and dividers against the pattern (see the photos on p. 50). Also, you can hold the pattern against the rounded blank, like a story stick, to mark the position of turning elements. Another advantage is that you can compare duplicates against the pattern. If you compare duplicates to each other, any errors made in the early duplicates will be compounded in the later ones. I make

Full-size pattern is the key. This step is worth every minute. Taking the set-up time to mark the turning lines prominently on the blank will help you avoid costly mistakes.

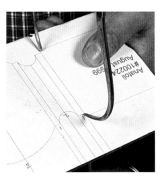

A pattern is a map and a story stick. You can use a full-size drawing of the workpiece to set calipers and to monitor your progress after you start turning.

Make it simple with a system of numbers. The author codes his calipers to correspond to different finished diameters on the workpiece.

patterns using a computer drawing program, but as an alternative you can use graph paper, a ruler, triangle, compass, and French curve set.

Paste the pattern, whether printed or drawn, to a thin but stiff piece of material. I use Masonite® or lauan because it's cheap, and I usually have plenty of scraps. Cut the scrap into a rectangle so that the top and bottom of the drawing correspond to the ends of the scrap. Orient the drawing so that the end going into the headstock is toward your left. Draw "turning lines" for all of the major and minor diameters to function as a story stick, marking the position of the spindle's turned shapes on the rough blank.

Number the turning lines so that those with the same diameters have the same number. The spindle illustrated here has eight diameters. Holding your calipers against the pattern, match each of the calipers to each of the different diameters on the pattern. For easy reference when I'm turning, I put masking tape on all of the calipers to be used and number them to correspond to the numbers on the pattern. For the eighth diameter, at the bottom of the spindle, set a pair of dividers instead of a caliper. (The sharp point on the dividers will score the end grain of the foot, showing

you where to stop the taper.) Altogether, for this pattern, you'll need seven calipers and one pair of dividers. With your pattern complete and your calipers set, you are ready to duplicate.

Mill the blanks

This design calls for 4-in.-thick mahogany. The thickest kiln-dried mahogany commercially available is 16/4, which is 4 in. in its roughly milled state. However, to cut the pommel accurately, the blank must be jointed and planed square, so this project requires a larger blank that can be planed to the proper dimension. In addition, turning is easier if the blank is slightly oversized. I glue up 10/4 stock to get a 5-in.-sq. blank and, when possible, use the same board for both halves of the blank for a good color match.

Joint the raw stock and cut it to length ½ in. oversized. Glue up the blanks. Don't scrimp on glue or clamps. Once the glue is dry, joint and plane the blanks. It doesn't matter how oversized the blanks are, as long as they're square and the same size. Set a stop on your saw and cut all of the legs to the finished length. Don't try to part the legs to length on the lathe because they won't all end up the same, and length is a critical dimension.

Some shapes
present challenges

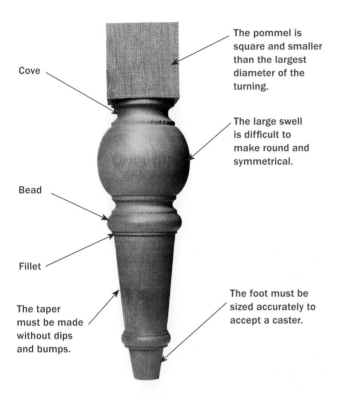

Cove

The pommel is square and smaller than the largest diameter of the turning.

The large swell is difficult to make round and symmetrical.

Bead

Fillet

The taper must be made without dips and bumps.

The foot must be sized accurately to accept a caster.

A custom straightedge. The knife edge of a mitered block of scrap will reveal high and low spots that need to be evened out. Backlighting helps.

A fine rasp for delicate cuts. Truing a tapered foot to fit into a brass caster is a good job for this tool.

Mark the centers on both ends of all the blanks, and mark the outline of the pommel on one of them. Cut the pommel's shoulders on the tablesaw, using a miter gauge with a stop. Cut out the pommel on the bandsaw, using a fence with a stop attached. Mark and cut the mortises. The blanks are now ready for turning. Mount the workpiece between centers and turn it to round. Watch the pommel—if you cut into it, the workpiece is ruined.

Transfer the pattern

Stop the lathe and hold the pattern against the blank. Then transfer the position of the turning lines to the workpiece. A quick flick of the pencil is all that is needed. Hold your pencil against the blank as you turn the lathe on and off, leaving pencil marks completely around the workpiece. Many experienced turners don't bother to stop the lathe. They simply hold the pattern against the workpiece while it's rotating and mark it. I stop and start the lathe because I've found that it's easy to damage the corners of the pommel when I don't.

Take the No. 1 caliper and—using a diamond-shaped parting tool—turn all of the No. 1 diameters. Don't put your finger through the caliper spring: If the workpiece catches the caliper, it could take off your finger. Continue parting with the remainder of the calipers. When you get to the No. 8 dividers, mark the end of the

Seven rules for duplicating parts

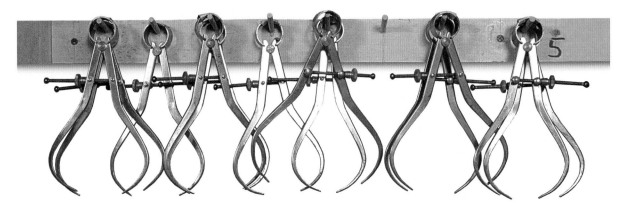

Concentrate on developing consistency rather than speed. If you work on consistency, speed will come. Some elements of consistency and speed are closely related. Here are my basic rules for achieving consistent results while duplicating parts on a lathe.

1. **Go as fast as you can without making a mistake, and no faster.** Speed comes from establishing and maintaining a rhythm. Making a mistake takes you out of your rhythm and slows you to a crawl. Once you've established a rhythm, look for ways to be more efficient. Try to push your-self. Increase your pace. Maintain your rhythm.

2. **Limit the size of your tool set.** Usually no more than three to five tools are needed for any given spindle—parting tool, skew, roughing gouge, one or two spindle gouges. Don't change tools unless you have to. Use one tool for different kinds of cuts

Hand drill as power sander. The author uses quick-change sanding discs in the final stages of shaping each leg.

(for example, I use a skew to turn the blank round and to turn beads).

3. **Limit movement of the tool rest.** The fewer times you stop to adjust the position of the tool rest, the faster the job will go.

4. **Use the same cutting sequence for each turning.** If you cut an element in three passes for the first spindle, cut it in three passes for subsequent spindles.

5. **Have enough calipers and dividers that you don't have to reset them.** These tools fall into the same category as clamps—you can't have too many of them.

6. **Learn to sharpen your tools freehand at the grinder.** Sharpening a tool shouldn't take more than 10 seconds.

7. **Power-sand where possible.** I mount sanding discs to quick-change bits so that I can change grits in seconds. Power-sanding is fast and also improves the finish markedly.

You don't need a wall full of tools. Gouges, a skew, and a parting tool were the only turning tools used to make the legs for this chapter.

workpiece simply by touching the left arm of the dividers to the end grain. This scored line will show the size of the small end of the tapered foot. (Don't touch the right arm, or it might snap over onto your fingers.)

Determine a cutting sequence for the turning

Whether you are establishing your diameters or turning the workpiece, always make your most difficult cuts first. That way, if you make a mistake you can't repair, at least you won't have invested much time. This spindle has four risky cuts, so I perform them in the order of their difficulty.

The square shoulder next to the pommel

On the leg shown on p. 51, the pommel will be covered by upholstery. But ordinarily, the pommel and its shoulders are highly visible. If you knock off a piece of the pommel, you'll have to repair it or discard the piece. This cut should be your first part when establishing diameters.

The large, round swell

After roughing, turn this element first. If you cut too many times and flatten the shape, you won't have enough material to recover. As you turn, compare the work to the pattern. I mount the pattern right behind the workpiece, so I just have to glance up to see it. It takes a practiced eye to see that the turning is different from the pattern. (Strangely enough, it's also hard to see when they're the same.) When the pattern and turning look the same, stop. Resist the temptation to take one last cut.

The large bead and the bottom bead

The large bead should be cut next because you must remove the material of the swell to get access to the material of the bead. Don't move the tool rest. Finish the coves, then the fillets on the top half of the workpiece. Move the tool rest to the bottom half of the workpiece and cut the bottom bead, which is the fourth risky cut.

Once you have established the diameters for the fillets at the top and bottom of the taper, you can eyeball the diameters of the top and bottom of the taper. I hold a straightedged pattern against the workpiece to see if the taper is flat (see the top right photo on p. 51).

You might suspect that the tapered foot is risky, but it isn't. Casters are forgiving in terms of sizing (length is more important than diameter) because they're held to the foot by screws. If you're trying to turn a tenon for a glue joint, size the tenon accurately by getting close with a skew, then finish up with a fine rasp (see the bottom right photo on p. 51). You can also make what's called a "go/no-go" gauge, so you know when you've just got it, by drilling the correctly sized hole in a piece of scrap.

Finish the work on the lathe

I usually power-sand the larger areas, then hand-sand the details. It's important that you don't oversand. It's easy to ruin the crisp details of a turning by rounding them over. As a last step, take a handful of shavings off the floor and hold them against the spinning work to burnish it, but keep your hands away from the sharp corners of the pommel.

You can apply a finish (shellac, lacquer, or oil) directly to the work while it's spinning on the lathe, but never wrap a finishing pad around your fingers or your hand. If it gets caught on the spinning workpiece, serious injury could result. You can achieve a French polish by building up shellac or padding lacquer against the spinning work.

Tips for Hollowing End Grain

ALAN LACER

End grain is the bane of many woodworkers. Furniture makers go to great lengths to hide it, and finishing end grain poses a number of problems. End grain can be just as ornery in wood turning.

Hollowing into end grain requires a different approach than hollowing into face grain. With a face-grain turning, a gouge is used in a cutting action that travels from the rim to the center. In this orientation, the bevel of the gouge rubs against the inside wall while cutting the wood fibers in the direction of the grain. However, a gouge does just the opposite when hollowing into end grain. Rather than laying down the fibers, it tears them.

To our benefit, wood turners have relied on a solution that dates back many centuries: the hook tool and its modern counterpart,

the ring tool (see the photo below). In essence, these two tools work like a bowl gouge with the flute bent to 90 degrees. Unlike a gouge, the hook or ring tool is used in a cutting action from center to rim. The cutting area and bevel are at right angles to the shaft of the tool, thus making it possible to rub the bevel against the wood as it cuts. A hollow center on the ring or hook tool provides a place for the wood chips to exit the cut.

Practice on a green-wood bowl

Hook and ring tools have a bad reputation because they are very aggressive and can catch easily. I find the best way to teach people how to hollow into end grain with these tools is to turn a shallow green-wood bowl. Green wood cuts much easier and cleaner than kiln-dried lumber, and bowls made with it can incorporate a natural edge that often will distort as it dries, adding an element of surprise to a design.

Two tools for hollowing into end grain.
The ring tool (top) is a modern version of the hook tool (bottom), which dates back centuries. Although they have some similarities to a bowl gouge, they cut from the center to the rim and have a cutting edge 90 degrees to the handle.

Another benefit of green-wood turning is that material is easy to find. I like to use freshly cut logs or tree limbs measuring anywhere from 3 in. to 12 in. dia.

Identify the center and mount the log

Most logs are not truly round. As a matter of fact, they come in about every shape other than square. So to incorporate a natural-edge rim successfully, you need to take some care when locating the center point. I use a shopmade template of Plexiglas® inscribed with different-diameter circles. I line up a circle with the perimeter of the log and then mark the center with an awl.

When first mounted between centers, the log will be off balance, so make sure it's on the lathe securely and that your lathe is set to a slow speed. Pound a four-spur center into the base end of the log and use a live-cup center to hold the rim end at the tailstock.

The first step is to face off the rim with a skew chisel. Unlike a parting tool, which tends to leave a jagged edge and tear the delicate bark, a shoulder cut with the toe of the skew will cut the bark cleanly.

Next, cut a round tenon on the base so you can remount the turning in a scrolling chuck. Use a skew chisel for this operation as well, making a series of peeling cuts by holding the flat of the skew against the tool rest and bearing down on the turning with the bevel

Start with a log or cut limb

A section of a small log or large tree limb is ideal for turning end-grain bowls with a natural edge. Mount the log on the lathe between centers to rough it round.

Turn a tenon on the base. Make a peeling cut with a skew chisel to cut the tenon.

Find the center. Lacer uses a clear plastic template with various diameters traced on it to help locate the center of the log.

Face off the top with a skew chisel. A shoulder cut with a skew chisel will make a cleaner cut in the bark than a parting tool.

Rough-turn the outside. Preserve a strip of bark for the rim and peel off the remaining bark before roughing.

of the tool. The tenon should be straight, and the shoulder above should be slightly concave to rest on top of the chuck jaws. Also, be sure the tenon isn't longer than the depth of your chuck. Next, rough-turn the exterior of the vessel, leaving a small patch of bark around the rim. Once you've completed the initial work between centers, take the turning off the lathe and remount it in the chuck.

Rough out most of the exterior

Several shapes will emphasize the natural edge. One is a flared rim—often described as a bell shape or a flower petal. Begin roughing out the exterior shape with a gouge. I use a heavy detailing gouge (½ in. across) or regular ⅜-in. or ½-in. bowl gouges. For this initial work, I still use the live-cup center on the tailstock end to keep it steady.

Cut most (two-thirds or so) of the outside shape before shifting attention to the interior. Also, turn the area around the delicate rim to a near finish, because it will be difficult to get a clean cut in this region once you've removed the supporting fibers on the interior.

Follow a strategy for hollowing

Begin hollowing by establishing a clean upper natural-edge rim, making light, shallow, slow cuts with a very sharp gouge from the rim toward the center. The tool may tear the fibers, but it is effective at removing waste rapidly, and the surface will be refined with the hook or ring tool. When you are satisfied with the rim, remove the tailstock center and drill a hole (½ in. or ¾ in. dia.) to establish the depth. This hole also removes the "stationary" center region and provides a start for the hook or ring tool. Then work the interior just below the rim with the hook or ring tool, cutting from the center to the rim.

Hollow out the inside

For the rest of the process, mount the tenon in a four-jaw chuck. Begin hollowing the center while using the tailstock center for extra support. Then remove the tailstock so you can cut deeper, alternating between the inside and outside of the turning.

Rough out the inside rim with a bowl gouge. This may cause tearout, but it is effective at removing waste quickly.

Switch to a ring tool or hook tool. Smooth the surface left by the gouge with either the ring tool (right) or hook tool (below). Cut from the center to the rim to produce a smooth surface. Hold the tool so that the flute is pointing between 9 o'clock and 10 o'clock.

Continue the roughing and smoothing process. Use a bowl gouge to remove material quickly, then a ring or hook tool to smooth out the final surfaces.

When the rim area is complete, continue hollowing the turning, first with the bowl gouge, working from outside to inside, and then with the hook or ring tool, making clean cuts from the center to the rim.

As you cut deeper with the hook or ring tool, hold the tool so that the flute is pointing between 9 o'clock and 10 o'clock, and take light to moderate passes. As you make the turn from the bottom up the wall of the turning, move the handle of the tool down and away from your body so that the bevel is always rubbing on the wood. If the bevel lifts, you run the risk of a catch. A catch also can occur if the angle of the flute approaches 12 o'clock.

When only the lower fourth of the bowl needs hollowing, shift your sights back to the exterior and turn it to its final shape. Then complete the inside with the hook or ring tool until the walls are uniformly about ¼ in. thick.

Scrape and sand to achieve a finished surface

To reduce sanding time dramatically, make the final passes on the interior of the bowl using a round-nose scraper oriented to make a shear cut. Hold the scraper tilted to about 45 degrees off the tool rest, pivoting on the left corner of the tool and cutting from the center to the rim. You'll know that you're

Turn to a final shape

Alternate between turning the exterior and interior until you've achieved a pleasing form with walls of a consistent thickness.

Scrape a finished surface. A rounded scraper tilted to 45 degrees generates a shear cut, which reduces sanding time.

Establish the outside shape. Use a detailing or bowl gouge to form the profile of the turning, always cutting in a downhill direction and with the grain.

Measure the wall thickness. Aim for consistently thick walls to prevent the wood from cracking as it dries.

Wet-sand on the lathe. Small turnings can be sanded on the lathe, using water and wet-or-dry abrasives ranging from 120-grit to 320-grit.

Part the bowl at its base. Cut off the turning with a thin-kerf saw (left). The remaining nub can be removed with a chisel or carving gouge. After the bowl has been dried, give it a final sanding (above) and then apply a finish.

holding the tool correctly if the cut produces long, thin shavings, as opposed to dust. Experiment with the cutting angle until it works.

Wet the entire bowl with a paper towel and sand with 120-grit through 320-grit abrasives. Then part the turning at the base with a skew chisel and cut it off with a thin-kerf saw with the lathe turned off. The base, which contains the pith of the tree, should be as thick as, or thinner than, the walls to prevent it from cracking as the wood dries.

Dry slowly and finish

To avoid cracks, slow the drying time by placing the bowl inside two heavy paper bags, or wrap it in newspaper and store it in plastic bags. Most of the drying—depending on humidity conditions—will take place in the first 48 to 72 hours using either method. For good measure, check the piece every day and change bags or newspaper regularly. If cracks

Sources

Ring tool
www.rockler.com
800-279-4441

Hook tool
Martel Hook Tool
martel.public.netc.net
amartel@netc.net
450-293-2186

start to develop, soak them with medium-viscosity cyanoacrylate glue. Give the piece at least 10 days of the paper treatment. After that, it should be ready for a final sanding and finish. I spray on a water-based, shellac-based, or lacquer finish for light woods and a wipe-on oil-based finish for dark woods.

Go Beyond the Lathe for Beautiful Vessels

JONATHAN BINZEN

The beautiful overall shapes Liam Flynn creates on his lathe immediately draw the eye. Yet much of what makes his vessels so memorable happens afterward. The signature double lip found on many of his pieces is made on the lathe but modified at the workbench. And all the fluting is done with the vessel off the lathe.

A lathe by nature generates perfectly symmetrical forms, but Flynn has found a way to produce turned vessels that are equal parts symmetry and asymmetry, perfection and imperfection. He may be aiming to find "the perfect line," but while he's pursuing it he lets the irregularities of work done by hand and by eye become part of the composition.

The double lip. Many of Flynn's vessels feature a distinctive double lip with an asymmetrical profile. He creates the lip partly on the lathe and partly at the bench.

Flynn turns and carves his pieces while the wood is still green—he chainsaws the blanks from sawlogs—so there is always some distortion of the overall shape as the piece dries. To minimize distortion, he cuts

Establishing the inner lip. After hollowing the vessel with a bowl gouge, Flynn uses a hooked scraper to define the shoulder of the inner lip. He uses the same tool to smooth the inside walls.

Last lathe step. Using a round-nosed scraper that's been ground back at an acute angle, Flynn shapes the recess between the inner and outer lips.

Faceplate leaves the lathe. Flynn turns all but the bottom inch of the vessel, then takes it to the bench for carving. He uses a shopmade jig (below) to hold it solidly in the vise.

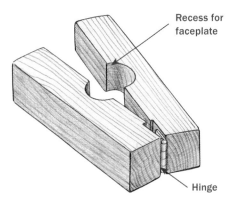

Recess for faceplate

Hinge

Slanting the lip. Flynn makes a sawkerf to provide a depth gauge as well as a relief cut (top) before carving down the outer lip. Working toward the kerf, Flynn uses a shallow gouge to cut an incline (above). Having reached the bottom, he does the same thing from the opposite direction.

out the blank so that the vessel's height is oriented perpendicular to the length of the log. He often turns the vessels from English oak (American oaks would be suitable, too), and he uses the prominent medullary rays as a guide while he's roughing out the turning: If he has it oriented properly, the rays should form vertical lines on two sides of the vessel.

Flynn begins a piece by screwing his blank to a faceplate and turning the outside form down to within an inch or so of the foot.

Then he hollows the inside and creates the double lip.

Now comes the carving. Flynn takes the vessel off the lathe but leaves it screwed to the faceplate—which he uses to help hold the vessel for carving. With most of the carving complete, Flynn removes the faceplate and mounts the vessel between centers to finish turning the foot. Then he completes the carving off the lathe.

Flute music. Flynn stays at the bench to carve the flutes. When most of the carving is done, he returns to the lathe to turn the foot, then completes the flutes.

Freehand fluting. Flynn cuts the flutes without layout lines preferring the slightly irregular effect it creates. When only a small space is left unfluted, dividers help him assess the width of the final flutes.

Back on the lathe. After unscrewing the faceplate, Flynn puts the vessel between centers on the lathe to turn the foot. The vessel is held between a cup center in the tail stock and a cylinder chucked into the headstock (above). He leaves a small spigot (right), which he removes later with a chisel.

Post production. To do the last bit of fluting, Flynn inverts the vessel on a cylindrical post clamped in a vise. Perfection is not his aim, Flynn says. "They're imperfect; that's the way it is. They're not machine-made." Certainly not.

Faceplate Turning Is Fun

JIMMY CLEWES

When it comes to turning, most furniture makers, not surprisingly, confine themselves to making furniture components. Regardless of the style, whether Shaker legs or period finials, almost all parts are turned between centers with the grain running parallel to the lathe's bed, a process known as spindle turning. However, there is another dimension to turning—faceplate turning—where the blank is attached just to the headstock end with the grain perpendicular to the bed.

Faceplate turning allows you to explore a whole new world of artistic woodworking, creating beautiful objects from start to finish in a few hours. Yet the tools and techniques are not that different from the ones you spindle turners are already familiar with. I'll demonstrate the steps involved by turning a platter, but a bowl is turned in the same way.

Freed from the conventional restrictions of furniture making, you'll find that turning stand-alone artistic pieces allows you to use a far wider range of wood. You only need an interesting chunk of a log, not a clear, 8-ft. section cut into boards and dried for a year. And in faceplate turning, the contrast between sapwood and heartwood is often prized, and irregularities like bark inclusions and burls are put on full display. However, you still want to avoid wood with cracks and checks in it, because the blank can fly apart. Although you can

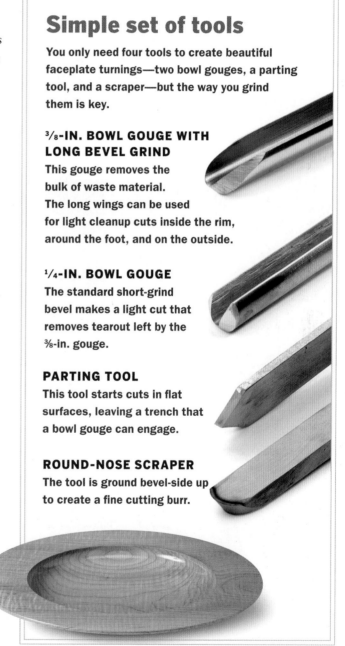

Simple set of tools

You only need four tools to create beautiful faceplate turnings—two bowl gouges, a parting tool, and a scraper—but the way you grind them is key.

³⁄₈-IN. BOWL GOUGE WITH LONG BEVEL GRIND
This gouge removes the bulk of waste material. The long wings can be used for light cleanup cuts inside the rim, around the foot, and on the outside.

¹⁄₄-IN. BOWL GOUGE
The standard short-grind bevel makes a light cut that removes tearout left by the ³⁄₈-in. gouge.

PARTING TOOL
This tool starts cuts in flat surfaces, leaving a trench that a bowl gouge can engage.

ROUND-NOSE SCRAPER
The tool is ground bevel-side up to create a fine cutting burr.

Grind a long bevel on a bowl gouge

Most bowl gouges come with a short bevel. To make it more versatile, Clewes grinds a long bevel that extends farther back. He uses Oneway's Wolverine sharpening system, set up as follows.

Place the gouge in the Vari-grind jig with its adjustable arm in the second stop from the bottom. Place the jig against the back of the V-arm support and extend the tip of the gouge until the base of the bevel is level with the front of the V.

Set the base of the jig in the V-arm and swing the jig back and forth until the wings are fully shaped.

turn green wood, in this case I used kiln-dried curly maple.

The basic sequence

The sequence for most faceplate turning is as follows: First, draw a circle on the wood using a compass. This not only gives you a line to follow on the bandsaw but also marks the center of the blank. After sawing away the waste, mount the blank with the outside or underside of the platter facing the tailstock. The simplest and most secure way to attach it to the lathe is using a faceplate, hence the name for this type of turning. Most lathes come with at least a small faceplate, but aftermarket plates in all sizes are inexpensive and easy to find. Next, shape the base or foot so that it can be attached to a four-jaw chuck (see "Four Jaw Chucks" on p. 22), and turn, sand, and finish the rest of the outside. Remove the workpiece from the faceplate and mount the base in the four-jaw chuck. Now you can turn and finish the inside and top of the platter.

Completely finish the outside first

The first thing to consider when turning the base of your platter is how you want the jaws of the chuck to grip the workpiece. They can either apply pressure outward against a recess or inward against a spigot. I prefer a recess because I think you get a better grip. The diameter of the recess will determine the size of the foot, and so it should be in proportion to the rest of the piece. About a third of the total radius is a good rule of thumb. If you are turning a recess with a foot, as I am, never make the outside of the foot the same depth as the recess (see the drawing on p. 66). If you do, you will end up with a potentially weak ring of wood on the base of the platter, which may break out when hollowing the inside.

The recess must be cut as accurately as possible so that the jaws of the chuck sit perfectly. It only needs to be deep enough to enclose the serrated ends of the jaw (see the bottom right photo on the facing page). I use a ⅛-in. parting tool to define the rim of the recess and a ⅜-in. bowl gouge to remove waste from the center. Feel free to use other tools you are comfortable with. Finish-sand the recess.

Mount the workpiece on the lathe and turn the foot. Screw on the faceplate to what will become the top or inside of the platter and then attach the faceplate to the lathe. Start by turning the outside of the blank round and the face flat. Then turn a recess that will accommodate the four-jaw chuck, used when shaping the inside of the platter.

Measure the chuck. When gripping a recess, four-jaw chucks have the most contact with the wood when the jaws are nearly closed. Set your calipers to that diameter.

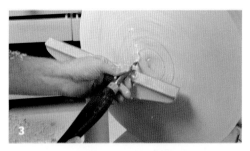

Lay out the recess. Use the calipers to mark the diameter of the recess on the spinning workpiece. Mark the outside of the foot, too, and then use a parting tool to cut the shoulder.

Complete the recess. Use the long-grind ⅜-in. bowl gouge to remove the rest of the waste from the recess.

Grip with the tip. There is no need to create a recess that matches the full depth of the chuck's jaws. Only the serrated tips need to grab the wood.

Profile the outside of the piece

With the recess and foot complete, it's time to shape the rest of the outside. Simple shapes please me most and my favorite is the softened ogee, which is attractive to the eye.

Don't turn at an excessively slow speed. Once the blank is balanced, higher speeds lessen the resistance of the cut and produce a better finish from the tool. To shape the outside of the platter, work from the center to the edge, going with the grain. I remove the bulk of the waste material with a ⅜-in. long-grind bowl gouge (see "Simple set of tools" on p. 63).

When you have shaped the outside of the platter, there will almost certainly be some

Rough out and refine the bottom

Use a series of tools to quickly shape the overall profile, and then produce a smooth surface with no tearout.

PROFILE FOR A PLATTER

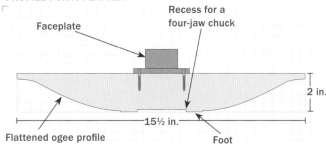

Faceplate

Recess for a four-jaw chuck

2 in.

Flattened ogee profile

15½ in.

Foot

Smooth it. Use the ¼-in. bowl gouge to make a single pass from the foot to the edge of the platter. If you go slowly and remove very little wood, the surface will have almost no tearout.

Rough it. When shaping the outside of the workpiece, cut from the center toward the edge, going with the wood fibers. Use the ⅜-in. bowl gouge. The side bevels, or wings, on the gouge can be used to make light, shaving cuts to clean up the surface.

tearout on the end grain. There are a couple of steps to take care of this. Make a finishing cut with a ¼-in. bowl gouge, also cutting from the center to the outside and removing only a little wood—up to ³⁄₃₂ in. The more even your movements, the smoother the finish, but the odd ripple can be removed by the next step.

Scrape it. Use the burr on a round-nose scraper to clean up the surface prior to sanding.

Shear-scraping, which is really shear cutting, leaves a surface that needs very little sanding. When preparing the scraper, try sharpening the tool upside down. This produces a longer, more even burr, as the grinding wheel draws the steel away from the tool edge. By the way, when the burr is worn away on one part of the cutting edge, a slight adjustment in tool angle will give you a fresh burr to work with.

Take your time sanding

The outside of the platter should be ready for sanding. I start with P180-grit paper and work through P240, P320, P400, and then CAMI 600, 800, 1,000, and 1,200 wet-or-dry paper, used dry.

The first sanding is the most important—any tool marks or disturbed grain should be sanded out to leave an even surface. If you can see any light lines in the piece, they are probably areas where the grain has been disturbed and they show up because dust has entered the disturbed grain. These lines must be sanded out before you go to the next grit.

I usually power-sand using small hook-and-loop-backed sanding disks attached to a corded drill. This speeds things up dramatically and gives better control and more even pressure. If you see the disk detaching itself from the pad, you are probably spending too much time sanding with too fine a grit and creating too much heat. You will be better off dropping back to a coarser grit.

When satisfied with the initial sanding, go through the grits, removing the sanding marks made by the previous abrasive. By the end, the wood should be polished enough to see your fingers reflected in it before you apply any finish.

Seal and then apply a finish

I finish my platters with Watco® Danish Oil, my favorite finishing product. It is extremely durable, with just the right amount of body, and it allows you to re-oil items later to rejuvenate them, providing you didn't apply a topcoat of paste wax.

However, don't apply the Danish oil to bare wood. On figured wood in particular, you would have to saturate the wood before you'd get an even sheen. Instead, seal the surface with either dewaxed shellac or an oil-based sanding sealer. Once dry, smooth the surface with Liberon's 0000 steel wool. Use a fine-weave, lint-free cloth such as an old T-shirt to apply the Danish oil in a circular motion with the piece stationary on the lathe. If you

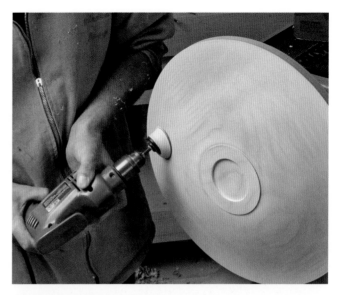

Finish before flipping. Take this opportunity to completely prep and finish the bottom of the platter. Although you can use sheets of sandpaper or random-orbit sander disks, the fastest and most effective way is to use hook-and-loop disks and a foam backer pad attached to a drill while the workpiece spins at a moderate speed.

Seal and steel. After sanding, seal the surface with shellac or sanding sealer. When dry, smooth the surface with good-quality 0000 steel wool.

see any white dots, they are pores filled with dust; apply more oil to these areas until they disappear.

Remove any excess oil using a clean cloth with the lathe turning slowly. Let the oil dry for about a half-hour before buffing to

A flawless finish. Because you sealed the wood first, the subsequent oil-based finish leaves an even sheen.

The first task is to flatten the face of the workpiece and bring it to the desired thickness. When laying out the inside of the platter, bear in mind that the width of the rim looks good if it is about one-third of the radius. Make a cut with a parting tool to define the rim edge. This will also serve as a shoulder for the bevel of your bowl gouge when you start hollowing the center.

Finish the rim first, leaving the bulk of the wood in the middle for support. I also divide the rim roughly into thirds with the outer third sloping toward the outer rim while the inner section slopes toward the inner rim but terminates in a kind of very small ski jump. This gives your fingers something to register against when you handle the platter. You also will be cutting downhill with the grain. I shear-scrape if necessary as I cut the wood, ready for sanding.

To remove waste from the inside of the platter, I again use the long-grind bowl gouge and the ¼-in. bowl gouge for the finishing cuts, working from the outside to the middle, as this is the way the grain is running. I erase any ripple marks by shear-scraping. Make sure the inside profile of the platter is a nice continuous curve with no hump or depression in the middle, a common oversight. To detect any discrepancies on the inside profile curve, simply use the tips of your fingers and run them back and forth over the surface; it's surprising how sensitive they are and how fine a flaw they can detect. When satisfied that everything is in order, sand, seal, and finish the inside in the same way as you did the outside.

a satin sheen with a clean cloth. Second and third coats are optional based on the sheen you desire.

Remount the piece and turn the inside

Now to the inside of the platter. Remove the faceplate from the unfinished side of the platter and screw the four-jaw chuck to the lathe. When mounting the piece in the chuck, make sure you put pressure right in the center of the workpiece. This will ensure that it is sitting squarely before the chuck jaws are tightened. Tighten until there is just a little resistance on the jaws, enough to hold the workpiece securely but not enough to dent the recess.

Flip and regrab. With the outside finished, remove the faceplate and use the recess you turned in the base to mount the platter on the chuck.

Rule of thirds. The rim should be about a third the radius of the platter. Use a parting tool to define the inside edge, and then divide the rim itself into thirds to help determine its profile.

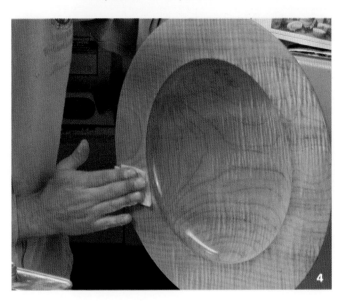

Turn the inside last
When turning the inside, reverse the process and work from the edge to the center.

PROFILE FOR A PLATTER

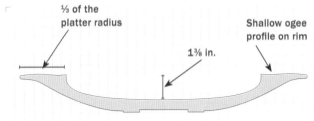

⅓ of the platter radius

1⅜ in.

Shallow ogee profile on rim

Work toward the center. Turn the rim using the same tools as the bottom of the platter, then hollow out the center. Weight in the center keeps the blank more stable.

The reward for good sanding. The oil-based finish will highlight any tearout or scratches, so don't skimp on the surface preparation.

Secrets of Segmented Turning

ART BREESE

It was golf that drew me to Sun City West, a huge active-retirement community outside Phoenix. But there are only so many rounds a guy can play, and I soon wandered into the woodworking club there. An amazing sight awaited me: 7,000 sq. ft. of first-class equipment and bench space, and dozens of people working away happily.

After doing a few projects on my own, I noticed a couple of people making segmented bowls, having fun and sharing knowledge.

They were extremely helpful in getting me started.

I quickly became an addict. When you make segmented turnings you are never in full control. You can sketch out a perfect plan for the segments, angles, and glue-ups, but you don't know exactly what you are going to see until the last surface is sculpted. In our shop, we think of a first attempt at

Clever tips and jigs unlock these puzzles in the round.

any design as a prototype, knowing we can improve on it the next time. That's the fun: striving for perfection, never quite achieving it, but always showing improvement.

And you don't need a big lathe or special accessories to do it. A combination disk/belt sander is very helpful, though.

Start with a precise plan

Obviously, an almost infinite array of glue-ups can produce an infinite variety of patterns. But there are two main types of assemblies, rings and staves, often combined in more complex vessels. I'll stick with the ring method here. It is the most basic approach, yet very versatile.

The first step is to decide on the patterns you want in the finished turning. You can base your design on photos of other people's work, or on your own brainstorming and sketches. Then you need to make a scale drawing to sort out the rings and segments needed. The segment angles are pretty standard. You just divide the number of segments into 360. However, to get the length and width of the segment blocks, you need an accurate cutaway side view of the bowl (see above). That will show you the width and thickness of each segment, but you still need the segment lengths. The simplest way to determine that is to take the circumference of each ring (π times its diameter) and divide by the number of segments. That will get you close enough, but the two methods on p. 72 are a bit more precise.

I chose an understated yet elegant walnut bowl for this introduction to the craft, throwing in a bit of contrasting holly to add flair: alternating segments in the lowest ring, outlined by holly veneer above and below, and more holly veneer sandwiched between the other segments, highlighting them with a fine contrasting line. So you'll

Start with a side view

A full-scale cutaway side view of your bowl will give the thickness and width of each ring. Then there are a number of ways to generate the length of each segment needed (see "Two ways to size the segments" on p. 72).

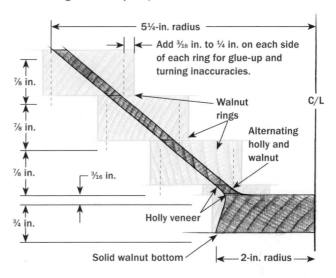

need to subtract 0.030 in. from the length of each segment to account for one thickness of veneer.

Precise jigs produce precise segments

Once you know the dimensions of the segments and you've chosen woods and decided how the grain should run, prepare the stock. Prep enough for a few extra segments. This is pretty standard woodworking, though you need to get everything perfectly straight and square, and be certain that all the stock for a given ring is planed to precisely the same thickness. The tricky part, as you might imagine, is getting all the angles right.

My main jig for cutting angles is a tablesaw sled, with a fence that can be set at common segment angles. With a sharp blade and an accurate sled, you can get good glue surfaces right off the tablesaw. If you are having

Two ways to size the segments

DOWNLOAD SOFTWARE
To get the size of any type of segment in any type of vessel, Breese recommends using a computer program. He and his friends use Table Saw Miter Angles (www.TurnedWood.com).

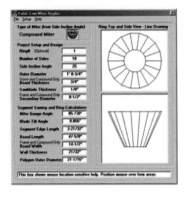

OR DO SOME GEOMETRY
Here's a graphic way to create a top view of the segments in this basic bowl. Set a compass to the inside and outside diameter of a particular ring (right). Then swing arcs around a centerline (center).

1. Set compass to outside edge at top and strike an arc.

2. Set compass to inside edge at bottom and strike an arc.

Centerline

Now use a protractor to define the angled edges and get the segment dimensions. (Each ring has 12 segments. Divide that into 360° to get the overall segment angle.)

Centerline

Segment length

Segment width

---

trouble, or if you are using a lighter wood that shows glue joints more obviously, you'll want another helpful jig for segmented turnings: an angle jig for the disk sander.

Be sure to cut a few extra segments and deburr the edges of each segment so they'll join cleanly.

Assembly starts with the base blocks

The first assembly step is screwing the waste block to the faceplate and then doing some light turning to clean it up. Start with the outside diameter. You'll do this for all the layers, which will help you keep them concentric and the vertical gluelines aligned nicely. Now turn the critical glue surface on the face. I use a round-end scraper to turn it as flat as possible, before relieving the center about ⅛ in., leaving just a 1-in.-wide ring around the perimeter. This gives the excess glue somewhere to go when you rub the joint together and put it into the clamping press. It also makes the bowl easier to part off later. Last, I press a board covered with sandpaper against the face to ensure it is dead-flat. I do this each time I am truing up a new layer on the lathe.

Now glue on the first layer of the bowl, the solid block that will form the bottom. On this and all the rings that follow, the glue face must be dead-flat, which I take care of on a belt sander (see middle left photo on p. 74).

To glue on each new ring, I turn to a setup that resembles a small veneer press. These can be made pretty easily from wood or metal. You can also use clamps and cauls, but you'll have to be very careful to balance the clamping pressure.

After a half hour or so for the glue to set up, you can turn that block to get it ready for the first ring. Again, clean up the outside diameter, turn the face flat, turn a shallow

Tablesaw sled produces perfect segments

The fence on this sled has a fixed pivot point, with precise holes drilled to bolt down the other end at common segment angles. To figure out a hole location for a specific angle, clamp the fence temporarily and cut test segments until you get a perfect ring, then drill a hole through the fence and base at the same time to lock in that angle for the future.

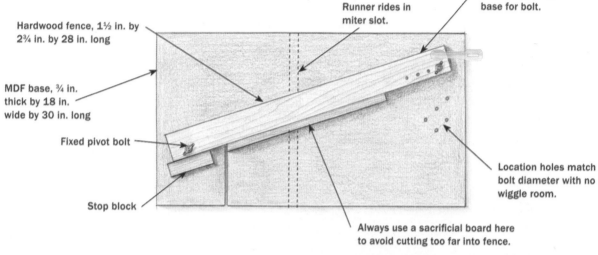

Hardwood fence, 1½ in. by 2¾ in. by 28 in. long

MDF base, ¾ in. thick by 18 in. wide by 30 in. long

Fixed pivot bolt

Stop block

Runner rides in miter slot.

Clamp movable end in place for test cuts, then drill through base for bolt.

Location holes match bolt diameter with no wiggle room.

Always use a sacrificial board here to avoid cutting too far into fence.

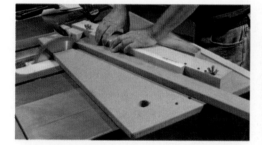

Cut one clean edge. After setting the fence at 15 degrees, the first step on the sled is simple. Move the stop out of the way and cut a clean angle on the end of the stock.

Set it and forget it. Now you can flip the workpiece and set the stop for the length of the outside of the segment. The stop stays put: You just flip the stock between cuts. Breese's clever hook-like holddown keeps the segment safely in place against the stop.

Check your work. To check the angles, dry-fit all 12 segments and pull them together with a hose clamp.

Rub joints make rings. These angled pieces would be difficult to clamp tightly, but rub joints work wonderfully. Glue up one pair at a time. Put glue on all mating surfaces (including the holly veneer between the upper segments), put the pieces down on a flat, nonstick surface, and start rubbing them firmly together. When the joint tightens, align the corners before setting the assembly aside. When it's dry, join the pairs until you have half-rings.

Sand the halves flat. This removes excess glue and any unevenness. Breese does this on a stationary belt sander using a light touch. (The pencil lines are for the next step.)

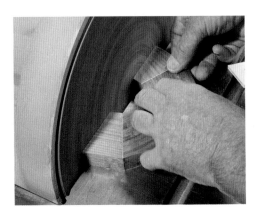

Now sand the edges. The disk sander ensures that the final rub-joint is gap-free. Watch the pencil lines to track your progress.

depression in the middle, and then apply the sanding block to ensure flatness.

For this design, the first layer of holly veneer goes on now. I cut it to size by placing what I've turned so far on a sheet of veneer, tracing around it, and then cutting it out with scissors. Then I clamp it in the press and let the glue cure for an hour or so.

Build the rings, segment by segment

It would be next to impossible to clamp all the angle blocks together accurately to form the rings. The solution is the humble rub joint. If your surfaces are clean, these joints

After joining the rings, sand again. Breese spins these lightly on the belt sander, but if you don't have one you can do your flattening on a big piece of sandpaper stuck to a flat surface as shown.

Build from the base up. The waste block goes on first. Screw a block of solid wood onto the faceplate and then prep its face for gluing. True up the outside diameter, and then skim the face with a round-end scraper before turning some relief (as shown) in the middle for glue squeeze-out.

Make a small press. To glue the rings together evenly and accurately, you'll need a small press like the one Breese and his friends made. Theirs is welded steel, but you can easily make one from hardwood and melamine, using a press screw.

9-in. press screw

Add the bottom of the bowl. This is a solid block of walnut, sanded flat. Always rub layers together first to create a thin glueline before clamping them in the press.

Now a layer of holly. Holly veneer frames the ring of alternating holly and walnut. Trace around the turning onto the veneer, cut out the disk leaving about ⅛ in. of excess, and then glue it on using the press.

Trim the veneer. A quick touch with a gouge removes the excess.

are very strong, and they also leave extremely thin gluelines, which look best. These tight joints also cure quickly, reducing downtime.

The key here is keeping each little assembly flat so the glue joint will be good, and the segment corners aligned so you ultimately get a round ring. If it isn't round, it will be impossible to align the segments vertically in the various rings.

My trick for ensuring flatness and alignment is simply holding the pieces against a 12-in.-by-12-in. granite plate as I rub them together. You could use any flat surface for this, such as MDF or melamine. You align the corners at the same time. For the first ring, you'll be alternating holly and walnut segments. Put a layer of glue (I use Titebond II®) on both mating surfaces, press them down on the plate, and rub them together until you feel the joint begin to grab. Be sure the corners are aligned before putting them aside to cure for 20 min. or so. Then join sets of pairs, wait, and so on until you have two halves of the ring.

Before joining the halves, they need some prep work. Sand their bottom face to remove the excess glue, and then bring them to the disk sander to sand both ends at once. This is another great trick from my friends at the woodworking club. Even if your segment angles were a little off, sanding the halves ensures that the final glue joints are tight. The trick here is to scribble on the ends with pencil, and then sand until the lines disappear.

Now you can rub the final joint together to complete the ring, and after one hour (to let the glue cure more fully), re-sand the bottom side of the ring to be sure it is still flat.

The only twist with the other rings is the little pieces of holly veneer that go between the other segments. You'll need to cut the pieces in advance (about ¹⁄₃₂ in. oversize is fine) to fit the glue faces of the segments, and then bond a piece between each segment as you rub them together. Don't worry, the veneer won't prevent you from eyeballing the corners of the segments to align them.

One layer at a time

You might be tempted to glue all the rings together at once, but don't do it. The pieces will slide around as you apply pressure and you'll never get them to stay aligned. Put on the layers one at a time, as we have been doing: Let each joint set up, and then clean up the outside of each one to get ready for the next.

At this point, the holly veneer is flat as is, but the outside diameter still needs to be trimmed on the lathe. After doing that, the "feature" ring (alternating holly and walnut) goes on. Use the rubbing action to remove the excess glue, and then put it in the press. Remember that one more layer of holly veneer goes above the feature ring.

As you add layers, pay careful attention to the vertical alignment of the segments in each successive ring. To be sure I bisect each segment, I mark centerlines. Then I position the ring properly and trace around it to be sure it doesn't shift as I am rubbing and clamping.

Each ring only needs 45 minutes or so to set up, but let the whole assembly cure fully overnight before turning the bowl.

Turn it and see what you've got

Start with the inside when turning the bowl. I recommend using a template, made from your drawing, to make sure you are turning close to the right angle or curve. You don't want to go too far and not have enough left outside to produce an even wall thickness. Then you can turn the outside, using a caliper on the walls.

Rings become a bowl. True up each ring as you go. Turn the outside to make it concentric, and then flatten the face with a round-end scraper again. Breese also sticks sandpaper to a board and uses that as a last flattening step.

Keep them aligned. It is critical that each ring stay centered and aligned properly in the press. Breese marks centerlines on the ring and then traces around the turned assembly to be sure it doesn't shift.

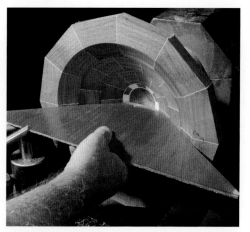

Turn the inside first. Turn until you have a smooth wall, and then check your progress with a simple template made from your drawing. You want to be sure you don't go too far and that the angle is right.

Now the outside. Just use a caliper to keep the wall thickness even, and your bowl should be perfect.

As for sanding and finishing, I go from P150-grit up through 600-grit, finishing up with 0000 steel wool. Apply your finish before separating the bowl from the faceplate and waste block. I use five or six coats of Minwax® Wipe-On Poly, using the 600-grit paper or 0000 steel wool between coats.

The bottom of the bowl is still attached to the faceplate, so the last step is to part the bowl off the waste block and finish turning the bottom. There are a number of ways

turners hold a bowl in the reverse position. I use a vacuum chuck at our community shop, but I'll demonstrate a lower-tech method using a shopmade plate (see the bottom photos below). I hollow my bases to help prevent rocking, and add a few decorative details.

After you sand and finish the base, you are done. There are lots of steps, but none of them hard, and once you get set up to turn segmented work, you'll become as addicted to it as I am!

Keep it on the lathe. Sand and finish the top of the bowl, outside and in, while it is still spinning on the faceplate.

Part it off. Breese got some help here from a white-gloved friend, who let the bowl spin in his hands and then caught it when it came free.

Reverse turning. You need to flip the bowl around to finish off the bottom. A vacuum chuck will hold it nicely, or you can make a simple faceplate as shown. Breese turned a channel in MDF to fit the rim of the bowl exactly, and then screwed on small wood tabs to hold it in place.

Works like a charm. The bowl spins true and holds fast, allowing Breese to face off the bottom, hollow its center a bit, and then turn a few nice details before sanding and finishing this last area.

Making Split Turnings

PHILIP C. LOWE

Split turnings have been incorporated into furniture since the 17th century and continue to be used as ornamental details in modern designs and reproductions. As the name suggests, these elements are turned round and then split into segments. Most often, split turnings are applied to the facade of furniture or buildings.

I have worked on a few antiques that incorporate incredibly fine split-turned elements. Some featured half-round turnings as surface decorations, whereas quarter-round turnings often decorated the interior or exterior corners of a piece. There are examples of other fractions of a round. Three-quarter turnings, for instance, were adopted in architecture to serve as "bumpers" to protect the outside corners of walls.

For the most part, early split turnings were turned round and then sawn apart by hand—a precarious job, to say the least. After the turning was split, the maker handplaned the back side and applied it to furniture. This technique is apparent in many museum pieces on which half-round split turnings are not exactly half round. The modern process is more reliable and involves far less risk of making a mistake. Dimensioned parts are glued into a single turning block, or billet, with a piece of kraft paper between each joint. After the billet has been turned on the lathe, it is split apart at the paper joints, which produces matching parts.

Add a layer of paper to the glue joints

To make a quarter-round split turning, glue up four segments that are equal in width and thickness into a billet. Between each segment place a sheet of brown kraft paper, which will provide a secure bond for turning on the lathe but will make the joint easy to break after the billet has been turned. The paper should be of medium to heavy weight (40 lb. to 75 lb.). The thicker or heavier the paper, the easier the billet will be to split. I often use recycled brown packing paper or grocery bags.

Apply glue to the surfaces of both adjoining segments. You can think of the paper as a very thin piece of veneer: It must have a glue bond with both segments. Water-soluble adhesives, such as hide, white, or yellow glue, work best because they are easy to remove after the parts are split.

Glue up in stages

Quarter-round split turnings require two stages of glue up. First, glue up two pairs of quarter segments with paper in between, and then plane a flat surface on each piece.

Half-round

Half-round. The facade of this 17th-century reproduction cupboard by Bill Brown features half-round split turnings.

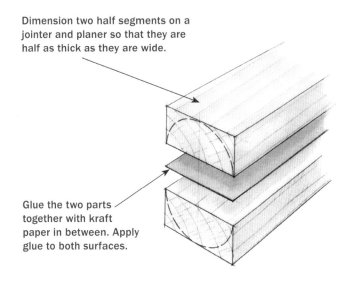

Dimension two half segments on a jointer and planer so that they are half as thick as they are wide.

Glue the two parts together with kraft paper in between. Apply glue to both surfaces.

Quarter-round

Quarter-round. This serpentine chest of drawers by Steven Franklin illustrates how quarter-round split turnings are used on exterior corners.

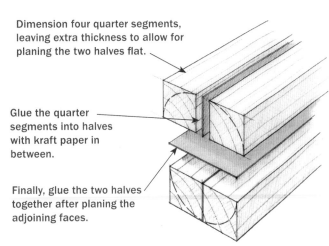

Dimension four quarter segments, leaving extra thickness to allow for planing the two halves flat.

Glue the quarter segments into halves with kraft paper in between.

Finally, glue the two halves together after planing the adjoining faces.

piece. Follow the same gluing procedure to assemble the two halves into the final turning billet. When preparing the stock for quarter segments, you can dimension the pieces so that they are slightly thicker than they are wide. That way, when they are glued up into halves, you can plane one surface flat and run it through the thickness planer to make the surfaces parallel. Providing this extra material from the start allows you to remove material and still come up with a square piece when the two halves are joined.

Follow the same basic steps when preparing split turnings of other fractions. For instance, half-round split turnings consist of two glued up pieces dimensioned so that the thickness is equal to half the width.

Center the billet on the lathe

Before mounting the billet on the lathe, drill a pilot hole in each end for the headstock and tailstock centers. If you drive the conical points on the centers into the ends without making pilot holes, the billet may split prematurely. This can make for an unsafe situation, as the billet has a greater chance of breaking apart and flying off the lathe

Glue up segments into a turning blank. For a quarter-round split turning, begin by gluing up segments in pairs. Apply glue to both surfaces and clamp them with a piece of kraft paper in between.

Handplane the surface of each half to remove any glue squeeze-out (top), and then glue up the halves with kraft paper between them (above).

while you are turning it. It's also important that the headstock and tailstock centers hold the billet as close to the middle as possible. Mounting the billet perfectly centered ensures that the pieces, once separated, will be exactly the same size. Use the intersection of the paper joints as a centerpoint. Also, if you use a spur center, don't align the spurs with the joints.

Turn with gouges and a skew chisel

Once the billet is mounted on the lathe, begin by rough-cutting a cylinder with a large flat gouge. Map out the profile of the design on a story stick and mark the locations of various elements (for example, the beginning and end of a cove) on the cylinder. A parting tool, along with calipers adjusted to the appropriate diameters, is used to turn any fillets or flats and to establish critical dimensions. I generally turn beads and quarter-rounds with a skew and use gouges of the appropriate size to cut the coves. I also use a gouge to cut a taper, or a slightly convex profile known as an entasis. The final step is sanding.

Clamp the halves. Make sure the glue is completely set before mounting the billet on the lathe, to prevent premature separation.

Remove from the lathe and split

When the turning is complete, remove it from the lathe. With the turning upright on a solid surface, break it apart with a stout mallet and the widest chisel you have. Place the cutting edge of the chisel on the paper joint. As you strike the chisel, angle it so that the bevel and the flat side of the chisel are at equal angles to the work and cleave the turning along the glueline. The fibers of the paper will begin to separate.

Finish the turning. Use a roughing gouge, a spindle gouge, a skew chisel, and a parting tool to turn the billet to its final shape.

Split with a chisel. Wedge the chisel into the glue joint and tap it carefully with a mallet until the turning begins to split apart.

As you drive the chisel farther into the turning, it may be necessary to rotate the chisel on its side to prevent the handle from hitting the workpiece. Continue to drive the chisel down the turning by striking the chisel on its edge until the segments pop apart. Try to restrain the halves so as not to drop and bruise them. Follow the same procedure to split apart the quarter segments.

Remove glue and paper before application

Wipe down the flat side of the turning with a damp cloth soaked in hot water to remove the excess paper and glue that remain. As the adhesive softens, scrape it off gently with a wide chisel, card scraper, or hook scraper. To speed things along, you can waft the glue surface with heat from a heat gun, but be careful not to burn the edges. Repeat this until all the residue is gone.

Apply a finish

You have two options for finishing. If you decide to apply a finish to the turning on the lathe before it is split, you will need to use a varnish or polyurethane product, which won't be affected by the water and heat used during the glue-removal process. You also can finish

Scrape away leftover glue and paper with a chisel. Drag the chisel over the surface with the bevel facing forward. Hide glue is easier to remove with water and heat than yellow glue, but either choice is fine.

the turning after it is split and clean of glue and paper. Temporarily mount the turning on the furniture piece with wood screws from behind or with double-faced tape. Mark the turning's location, then remove it and mask off the area to leave a clear spot where you will apply glue. Finish the furniture piece and the turning separately, and then glue the turning into place.

Fixing Turning Mistakes

ERNIE CONOVER

Sometimes repairing a turning mistake is a better option than making a replacement part. For example, there are times when you don't have extra stock for a good match (in figure and grain) to the rest of the piece. Other times, starting over can be a blow to your morale, not to mention time-consuming.

Fortunately, there are several methods for fixing both turning mistakes and flaws in the wood itself, whether you are doing faceplate work or turning spindles.

Don't be afraid to vary the diameter of multiple parts, such as table legs, if it means cutting away a mistake or defect. Fortunately, although the eyes are able to discern when elements are misaligned in height, they are much less sensitive to variances in diameter. To this end, the quickest way to fix a goof is simply to turn the affected area to a slightly smaller diameter, removing the flaw.

Every turning has a major diameter, which usually is the diameter necessary to turn the block you started with round, and a minor diameter, which is the narrowest part. As long as the major and minor diameters are made fairly consistent, a lot of variation can occur between other elements without being noticeable. And slight variances among major and minor diameters may be almost imperceptible.

With experience, you'll realize when you can get away with variations in diameter and when you can't. For example, the legs of a

Can you tell the difference? To conceal a mistake, the bottom spindle was turned to a slightly smaller diameter.

table can be off in diameter by as much as 3/16 in. because they are positioned so far apart. Turnings that are closer together, however, such as chair legs, will tolerate variances of only 1/16 in. or so. Beads are especially prone to blunders, but exact duplicates are not necessary to create an acceptable match.

Plane a flat and glue on a patch

When you can't get away with varying the turning diameter to mask mistakes, the most effective repair is to patch the damaged area with wood of the same grain and color. When turning new spindles, this is easy because you probably will have cutoffs of like wood on hand. When repairing older pieces, finding exact species, grain, and color to match can be difficult, and all of your finishing skills are subsequently brought to bear.

Flat patches

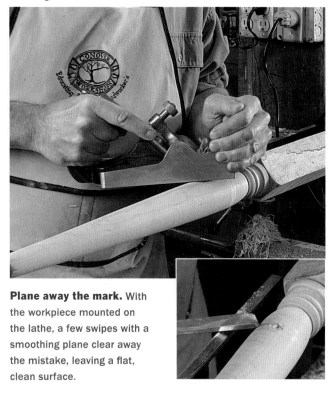

Plane away the mark. With the workpiece mounted on the lathe, a few swipes with a smoothing plane clear away the mistake, leaving a flat, clean surface.

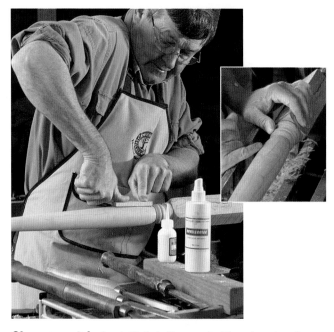

Glue on a patch. A cutoff of similar wood with a planed surface and matching grain is glued over the flat with cyanoacrylate glue (above). Pay attention to matching the grain, and a patch of this kind can go almost unnoticed after you re-turn the area (inset).

The easiest way to patch an area with new material is to flatten the damaged area with a smoothing plane and then glue a chunk of wood of like grain and color in place over the flat. I generally plane the workpiece on the lathe by locking the spindle, but sometimes I secure it between dogs on a workbench. The patch also must have one surface planed flat. Before gluing it in place, shape it on the bandsaw. Attach the scrap block to the flat with medium-viscosity cyanoacrylate glue and allow it to dry. Then re-turn the area and sand it smooth.

Drill and plug a mistake

Another patching method is to drill out the damaged area with a short hole and plug it with matching scrapwood. It's important to turn the plug so that the grain direction matches the repair area on the workpiece. When this type of patch is used in a spindle turning, it generally means faceplate-turning the scrapwood with a bowl gouge so that the end of the plug shows the cross-grain. One thing to note is that although this is called faceplate turning, you need not use a faceplate. The key is the orientation of the grain. A plug also is an excellent method of patching end grain, in which case the plug can be spindle-turned so that the grain runs between centers. Use a spindle gouge for this operation. Once the plug has been turned, glue it into the hole, trim it with a handsaw, and then turn it flush.

Patch the area with a ring of wood

Some repairs call for more complex measures. If a bead has been damaged beyond repair, it can be removed, and a replacement ring can be turned and fitted to the damaged area. That ring then is turned into a bead.

Start by cutting away the old bead, leaving a smooth cylinder. Next, make a ring with

Plugged patches

Drill away a deep gouge. With a Forstner bit, drill a ¾-in.-dia. hole into the blemish to make room for a plug.

A newel as good as new. Careful grain matching can create a patch that will be imperceptible once this newel post becomes part of a staircase.

Plug the hole. Using a chunk of wood from the scrap end of the newel post, turn a plug and glue it in the hole.

an inside diameter that matches the outside diameter of the cylinder. If this diameter is small enough and matches a drill bit, you can make the ring by drilling a hole into a piece of scrapwood. If the cylinder has a large diameter, you can turn the ring on the lathe. Once you have a well-sized ring, glue it over the damaged area and re-turn the bead.

Replacement beads

Cut away a botched bead. Then turn a ring with an inside diameter that matches the outside diameter of the spindle.

Glue the ring onto the spindle. The ring should fit tightly over the affected area (above). Then turn a new bead. Well-matched grain will make it hard to detect.

Fill a mistake with sawdust and glue

As my father would have said, "Without putty, paint, and glue, what would the poor carpenter do?" In wood turning, too, these materials can come in handy for patching and hiding mistakes and defects.

To fill a void left from a tear, gouge, or natural blemish, use cyanoacrylate glue, an industrial-grade super glue available at woodworking-supply companies such as Craft Supplies USA (www. woodturnerscatalog.com). Mixed with sawdust, the glue can make a blemish blend right in on a finished workpiece. Cyanoacrylate glue comes in three viscosities: water thin, medium, and thick.

Apply water-thin glue to the surface of the workpiece before beginning the repair. This

Sawdust filler

Patch a natural void. Tape the rim of the bowl to create a dam for a glue-and-sawdust patch.

Spray accelerator on the glue to speed the set time. It may take several layers of glue and sawdust to fill the void.

Once the area has been patched, re-turn the bowl. The repair is not discernible.

allows the patch to sink deep into the wood, ensuring that it holds well. Then sprinkle some wood dust and/or chips of the wood from your turning into the hole and apply medium- or thick-viscosity cyanoacrylate, depending on the size of the hole. With each application of dust and glue, spray the area with accelerator, which causes the glue to harden in as fast as 30 seconds, depending on temperature and the size of the patch. Stop filling when there is a bulge on the workpiece where there formerly was a hole. Then turn away the excess fill until the area is uniform with the rest of the surface. Finally, sand it smooth. I use this repair method more in faceplate work than on spindles. It is especially useful when turning bowls from green or dry wood.

For very large defects, use sawdust and five-minute epoxy, which is cheaper and faster than several applications of cyanoacrylate glue. The effectiveness of this patch varies greatly with the wood and circumstance. I also have used this technique to fill knots (especially ones with a loose piece still in place). Once it is sanded, I brush over the patch with India ink and apply finish after the ink dries.

Patch with a burn-in stick or putty

Burn-in sticks (which essentially are shellac with a bit of color added and then cast into sticks) are effective at patching minor defects or mistakes, such as small catches, pinholes, and small knots. There is no magic to patching with a burn-in stick; just melt the material into the hole and smooth it over with the hot tool as best you can. Avoid getting the burn-in stick so hot that it boils and turns blackish. For bigger defects, it is more effective to use two applications because burn-in sticks shrink as they cool. Quit when there is a slight bump on the workpiece where there used to be a dip. Then turn and sand the area.

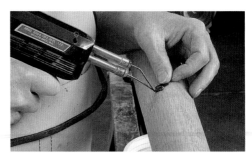

Melt on a patch. A soldering iron melts the burn-in stick onto the marred area. The defect then can be re-turned and sanded smooth.

Colorize Your Turnings

JIMMY CLEWES

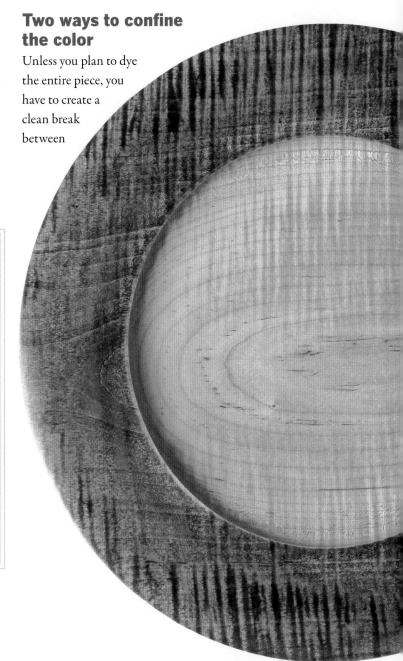

On many turnings, adding a bright dye can transform a competent piece of work that might not get a second glance into a piece of art that stands out from across the room. Wood turning is a creative craft, and coloring is an even more creative process. Even if you've never applied dye to furniture, I hope you'll break the bonds of inhibition and try dyeing a turning.

When it comes to dyes, my first choices are alcohol-based, and in particular those by Chestnut Products. These are pre-mixed and can be used at full strength or diluted with denatured alcohol. These dyes have a 5% shellac content, so each application progressively seals the wood. Therefore, the later colors soak in less and become more like glazes, creating a layered look rather than mixing into the previous ones.

Two ways to confine the color

Unless you plan to dye the entire piece, you have to create a clean break between

Alcohol dyes are brighter and dry faster

Compared with water-based dyes, alcohol-based ones are brighter and dry faster. You can buy them as liquids or as powders that dissolve in alcohol. Solar-lux liquids and alcohol-soluble dye powders are available at www.woodworker .com. You can view Chestnut Products dyes at www.toolpost.co.uk.

Seal adjacent areas. If you aren't going to dye the whole piece, wipe a washcoat of shellac onto the areas to remain undyed. Follow with Danish oil.

the dyed and undyed parts. The safest way is to turn and sand the whole piece, then seal the section that will remain undyed. In this case, I wiped a 1-lb. cut of shellac onto the platter's recessed center, and once that was dry, I applied a coat of Danish oil. If any dye seeps onto the sealed and oiled surface,

it comes right off with steel wool. On the other hand, avoid leaving either finish on the section to be dyed or you'll end up with a blotchy appearance.

If you are a confident turner, a quicker method is to turn and sand the area to be dyed, but leave some waste wood on the adjacent section. After the dyes have been applied and dried, come back and turn the rest of the piece, removing the unwanted dye at the same time.

Prep the surface and apply the dye

The surface must be flawless, because any blemishes will show up when you apply the dye. If you are using curly or burl wood (both give pleasing results), the grain may be running in different directions, so inspect the surface very closely. Use the same sanding method described in "Faceplate Turning Is Fun" on p. 63.

After the last sanding, raise the grain. I do this by spraying the surface with denatured alcohol because it evaporates quickly. Water works as well but takes longer to dry. Don't

Another way: Dye first, turn later

A more surefire way to get a crisp break between dyed and natural wood is to apply the dye and then complete the turning, cutting away unwanted dyed areas.

Finish the rim. Shape, sand, and dye the rim of the platter but don't hollow the center.

Finish the center. With the rim colored, use a parting tool to define the inner edge of the rim. Then finish turning the center.

Apply the dye. Starting at the inside edge, use the chuck to turn the platter by hand as you dye the wood.

A light sanding. When it's dry, sand the dyed area. You can then move on to the topcoat or add more color.

resand the wood; you want the dye to penetrate deeply.

Coloring is best done on the lathe: You can turn the piece slowly without touching it by revolving the chuck, and then turn on the power for sanding. Apply the dye with a brush, cloth, sponge, or folded-up paper towel, but be sure to cover the whole surface evenly and quickly because alcohol-based dyes dry in under a minute. If you do get streaking, quickly wipe the surface with an alcohol-dampened cloth.

Once the surface is dry, lightly sand it with CAMI 600-grit wet-or-dry paper. If you are satisfied with the appearance, you can go ahead with the clear coat or apply another coat of the same color.

Layers of color give a dramatic effect

After you've mastered using a single color, there are a couple of ways to use multiple hues. On curly wood, dyes penetrate the short grain more than the long grain. To exploit this effect, let the first color (in this case Chestnut Products' Royal Blue) dry completely, then sand the surface with CAMI 400-grit wet-or-dry paper. This step removes some of the color and leaves a striped effect.

Make the tiger roar. To enhance the stripes of the tiger maple, Clewes sands the first coat with 400-grit paper and then adds more color.

Bolder stripes. On the third round, instead of dyeing the whole rim, Clewes focuses on the darker sections of the curl.

Next, apply a lighter complementary or contrasting color, in this case a more turquoise blue, which will show most where the first blue was removed. Now sand the surface again, this time with CAMI 600-grit paper.

Soften the contrast. If you want the colors to flow slightly together, spray the piece with denatured alcohol. Don't wipe it off.

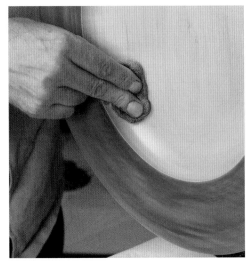

Easy cleanup. If any dye does get onto the sealed section, 0000 steel wool removes it.

Frame the rim. Coloring the edge of the platter with a permanent marker conceals any dye that bled through and provides a nice break between the dyed and undyed parts of the rim.

Quick finish. Gloss lacquer pops the colors, and using an aerosol gets the job done quickly.

You can either stop here or make the figure pop more with a third color. You can apply the third color to the whole area or just to certain sections. On curly wood, this can be just the lighter parts of the stripes, or on non-curly wood, you can use a dappled pattern. Continue coloring and sanding until you are pleased with the result.

A gloss finish brings the dye to life

Although I favor a low- or medium-luster finish for most of my undyed pieces, a thin, high-gloss finish really makes the dyes vibrant and the wood almost iridescent.

Although you could wipe or brush on a finish (don't use shellac or you'll pull and blotch the alcohol-based dyes), the easiest and fastest finish is spray lacquer. Use a spray gun if you have one, but for small projects like these, an aerosol is economical and won't leave you with a gun to clean.

Spray several light coats of lacquer, letting each coat dry for 20 to 30 minutes. Smooth the surface with CAMI 800-grit wet-or-dry paper followed by 1,000-grit and finally 1,500-grit. For a glasslike finish, buff the piece using liquid car polish.

Four Finishes for Turnings

TERI MASASCHI

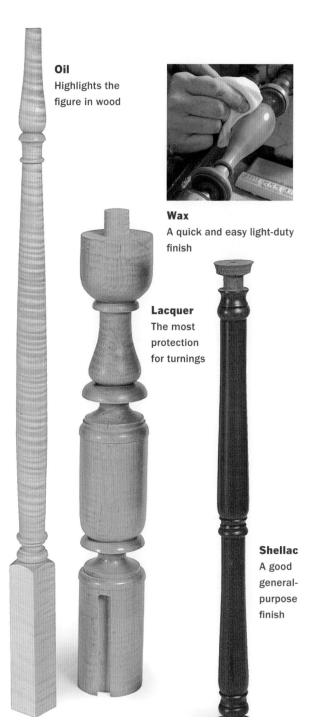

Oil
Highlights the figure in wood

Wax
A quick and easy light-duty finish

Lacquer
The most protection for turnings

Shellac
A good general-purpose finish

Wood that is spinning on a lathe allows the finisher to apply various finishes rapidly and flawlessly. Although most of the finishing materials used on turnings are familiar to wood finishers, the method of application is different. Sanding is far less of a chore, grain filling is quicker and less messy, and the friction caused by the applicator (usually a pad or cloth) dries the clear coating instantly. The problems of sags, dust, or other imperfections are simply nonexistent. In short, finishing turned work provides almost instant gratification.

Which finish works best?

Although the brand names are many, the actual categories of finishes used on turnings are few. The intended use of the turning is the key to choosing a finish: If it is a decorative object subject to occasional handling, such as a candlestick, shellac or wax would be fine. If it is a chair part subject to moderate wear, shellac or an oil finish are possibilities, whereas an item such as a kitchen-table pedestal needs a durable lacquer finish to resist shoe scuffs. Finally, salad bowls and other woodenware need food-safe materials applied to them, such as mineral oil, 100% tung oil, or some types of linseed oil (check with the manufacturer to make sure there are no added driers, which are toxic).

Sanding sponges protect fingers from friction heat. They're also flexible, which allows them to enter coves without dulling crisp shoulders.

Grain filler can be colored. Use a cloth to apply the filler to the spinning wood (above), forcing it into the grain and removing any surplus. Smooth the surfaces with a 4,000-grit Abralon pad (below) before moving to the next finishing step.

Some materials are initially applied with the wood standing still. Then, with the piece spinning in the lathe and a cloth held firmly against it, the surface is polished. Other materials are applied directly to the moving wood. They dry rapidly because of the friction and produce an instant gloss.

Before finishing, it's important to sand, fill, and stain

If your work has been properly turned, you should only have to start with 180-grit paper—usually much higher. I use standard aluminum-oxide sheets of sandpaper, but sanding sponges are a flexible alternative (see the top photo at left).

For most liquid finishes you can stop sanding at 400-grit because most of them involve some scuff-sanding during the application. But a wax finish requires a perfectly smooth surface. So, at 500-grit swap over to Abralon® pads, progressing through 1,000-grit, 2,000-grit, and 4,000-grit. Then switch to sheets of Micro-Mesh® abrasive, moving from 6,000-grit to 8,000-grit to 12,000-grit.

Most turning exposes a lot of end grain, which absorbs stain and finish differently

A moving stain. An alcohol-based dye or a pigmented oil stain is applied to the spinning workpiece in thin coats with a clean cloth.

than face grain, so you may need to deal with this problem before applying a final finish. Sanding up to 12,000-grit is one option to close up the pores and achieve an even finish penetration.

Instead, after a light sanding with 400-grit, you can use a grain filler. If you prefer a more open-grain look, glue size works well. Both grain filler and glue size can be applied while the workpiece is spinning in the lathe. The filler is forced into the grain quickly and smoothly with a rag, and the friction simultaneously removes the excess. The glue size is applied the same way. Both the filler and the glue size are dry to the touch in four to six hours. Once it's dry, you can jump right ahead to 4,000-grit to smooth and dewhisker the surface.

If you are going to color the workpiece, use an alcohol-based dye stain to achieve maximum transparency (water-based dyes gum up the glue size and some grain fillers). Or you can apply an oil-based pigment stain if you are more comfortable with this product. Application of either the dye or the stain is easier and will be more even if the wood is moving. Using a cloth, apply multiple thin coats until you reach the desired color.

A wax finish requires careful preparation

Wax finishes are available in solid or liquid form. The traditional method of applying wax to turnings has been to use solid bars of carnauba wax or blends made by Hut. Press the bars against the spinning wood to apply a thin but uniform coating, then burnish the surface with a tightly held cloth. Turn over the cloth frequently to expose a clean surface to the wood. Burnishing leaves a thin but smooth surface that brings out the flawless beauty of the wood.

New alternatives to solid wax are liquid shellac and wax mixtures, such as Hut's Crystal Coat or Shellawax cream by U Beaut Polishes. These generally are applied to the workpiece while it is stationary in the lathe and then burnished with a clean cloth while the workpiece spins. As with solid wax, the gloss appears almost instantly, leaving a smooth surface.

Shellac is a good all-purpose finish

Applying shellac to a turning is rather like French polishing in that multiple thin layers are applied over a short time. Instead of a special rubber (pad), a simple piece of cotton cloth is used as the combination applicator and burnisher. Because the shellac is applied

Solid wax. After holding the solid bar of wax against the moving section of a candlestick, burnish the surface with a clean cloth pushed hard against the wood.

Liquid wax. Apply the shellac/wax cream while turning the work by hand. Once all of the wood has been coated, turn on the lathe and buff the surface to a high gloss.

A moving finish. Apply the shellac by moving the cloth up and down the turning wood. The shellac dries instantly, allowing several coats to be applied in quick succession.

in such thin layers, you can afford to use a heavy 3-lb. cut. Avoid using shellac on items subject to constant handling, such as pens and walking sticks, because the acid in human hands can eat into shellac.

Lacquer is durable and quick to apply

Lacquer finishes, which include Behlen's Woodturner's Finish, Qualasole, and French Lac, all are applied with a lint-free cloth held gently against the workpiece while the lathe is running. There is no need to flood the wood because these film finishes are not meant to penetrate the wood.

For slightly open-grained wood or areas of exposed end grain, apply a coat of Myland's cellulose sanding sealer while the workpiece is stationary. After the sealer has dried, apply Myland's high-build friction polish using a lint-free cloth while the workpiece is turning.

When building a finish, occasionally stop the lathe to check whether the surface has any nibs. You can remove the nibs with a 4,000-grit Abralon pad.

Oil accentuates the figure in wood

Oil finishes, including Danish oil and Waterlox's® Original Sealer, are applied to the moving workpiece with a saturated cloth. Once the wood has been coated, hold a 400-grit sanding sponge against the spinning work, which pushes the oil into the wood, creates a slurry that fills voids, and leaves the surface slippery smooth.

Seal the surface. When finishing with lacquer, applying a cellulose sealer while the workpiece is stationary helps smooth the end grain.

Instant shine. After sealing the workpiece, apply lacquer to the moving wood to give an instant high-gloss look.

Oil also is a good choice for turnings or parts of turnings that can't be finished while the lathe is moving, including offset turnings, spiral turnings, and legs that have square shoulders. The oil can be applied and then sanded by hand with no obvious distinctions from the power-sanded areas.

Most food-safe finishes are oil based and require heavy penetration into the wood to be effective. For this reason, it is less messy to apply the oil liberally while the woodenware is off the lathe and allow the oil to soak in. If necessary, the piece can be remounted and the oil sanded in with 400-grit sandpaper or a sanding sponge. Food-safe finishes include tung oil, Waterlox Original Finish, mineral oil, and linseed oil that doesn't include metallic driers such as Tried and True oils.

Wipe on the oil. With the lathe off, apply the oil with a cloth, turning the workpiece by hand.

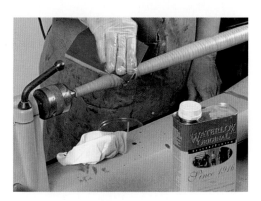

A penetrating finish. After oiling the wood, turn on the lathe and wet-sand the surface with a 400-grit sponge. This pushes the oil and sawdust slurry into the voids, smoothing the surface and enhancing the figure.

Spare the oil and spoil the bowl. Don't be afraid to flood the wood with a food-safe oil and let it soak in. Only in this way will the bowl survive future exposure to foods and dishwater.

Sources

FINISHES USED ON TURNINGS

Penn State Industries
www.pennstateind.com
800-377-7297

Woodcraft
www.woodcraft.com
800-225-1153

ABRALON PADS AND MICRO-MESH SHEETS

Micro-Surface Finishing Products
www.micro-surface.com
800-225-3006

Woodworker's Supply
www.woodworker.com
800-645-9292

Turned Drawer Pulls

PHILIP C. LOWE

When a project calls for turned knobs for drawers or doors, I always make my own. I hate paying for something I can make in my shop. But more important, making every element of a furniture piece, down to the knobs, brings a feeling of accomplishment that I don't get from using store-bought parts.

When turning knobs on the lathe, there are two basic methods to follow and a few different ways to add decorative elements. There also are some tricks for making matching knobs.

Turn long-grain knobs between centers

You have one initial choice when designing a turned knob. Should it be turned on a faceplate or as a spindle between two centers? Spindle-turned knobs are made with the grain running in the long direction and attach to the drawer face with a tenon. In this orientation, you can cut several knobs from one length of stock—ideal when a project calls for multiple matching knobs. This typically is the method I use to turn a knob with a narrow diameter.

Turn multiple knobs from one length of stock. Rough-turn between centers as many as four knobs from a blank. Then cut apart the blank to finish each knob individually.

Turn multiple knobs from one spindle

One popular example of a spindle-turned knob is the Shaker drawer pull. A number of classical profiles exist, but they don't vary a great deal. The one shown above consists of a tenon, followed by a fillet, an asymmetrical cove called a scotia, and a bead. Some refer to this kind of knob as a mushroom pull.

Begin with 4/4 stock and cut a piece of equal width and thickness. Each knob will require about 2¼ in. of material, so size the length of the material according to the number of knobs you want to make. But don't turn more than four knobs per spindle because it is difficult to create the narrow-diameter tenons on a piece that is too long; the pressure from the tool will create chatter. If I need more than four knobs, I'll turn them from multiple spindles.

Mount the spindle on the lathe and use a roughing gouge to turn a cylinder with a consistent diameter. Then mark off the location of each tenon with a pencil and turn down the area with a parting tool to the desired diameter. Choose a diameter that is equal to a standard drill bit, as this will make it easy to mount the knobs on the drawer fronts.

After each tenon has been turned to the correct diameter, cut a small chamfer with a skew chisel into the end of the tenon where

Rough out a blank to a common diameter. Then use a parting tool to turn the tenon end of each knob to the diameter of a standard drill bit. Calipers help achieve consistency.

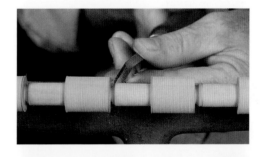

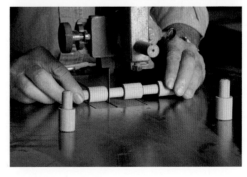

Separate the knobs. Use a skew to cut a small chamfer on the end of each tenon (middle). The chamfer helps guide the bandsaw blade as the knobs are cut apart (above).

Remount a knob blank. Clamp the tenon end in a Jacobs chuck and turn the base of the knob to a diameter greater than that of the tenon.

Mark for the cove and bead. Cut grooves at the pencil marks with a skew.

Turn the cove. Use a spindle gouge to turn the asymmetrical cove, also known as a scotia.

Round the face of the knob. A proper cut with the toe of a skew chisel will produce a smooth surface on the end-grain face of the knob (left). Then use the skew chisel like a scraper to clean off the button (right).

Sand and finish with the knob mounted on the lathe. Start with 150-grit and work toward 220-grit, wetting and drying between each grit. Burnish with a rag or the shavings from turning and apply a penetrating finish.

it meets the next knob on the spindle. This will make it easy to separate each knob. Remove the spindle from the lathe and cut off the individual roughed-out knobs at the bandsaw.

Separate the knobs for the finish work

With the chuck mounted in the headstock (I use a Jacobs chuck), insert the tenon end of a knob into the chuck and tighten it. Once you've determined the profile of the knob, mark the points where the fillet, cove, and bead will begin and end. You can do this with a pencil while the lathe is running.

Turn the knob to the desired profile, checking for consistency with calipers along the way. I use a parting tool to cut the flat, a skew to cut the rounded top, and a ¼-in. gouge to cut the cove. When you are satisfied with the shape, sand the knob to a final finish. I use 120-grit, 150-grit, 180-grit, and 220-grit sandpaper, wetting the wood with a rag and letting it dry between each grade.

To make additional knobs, follow the same steps and use calipers to match the diameters of each section to the first knob.

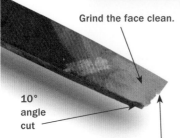

Grind the face clean.

10° angle cut

Half of rosette profile

Custom cutters. Make your own cutting tool by grinding a profile on an old file to reproduce a decorative cut on the face of a knob. The tool described here was made to cut a rosette pattern.

Customize a chisel to reproduce a rosette

Once you've mastered the basic knob, you may want to experiment with different styles and ornamentation, such as a rosette pattern. The trick is being able to reproduce the pattern on multiple knobs. One way to do that is to grind a cutter to match the profile of the decoration. For instance, to cut a rosette pattern I use a scraper custom-ground for that purpose (see the photos at left).

Make the cutter from an old, worn-out mill file. Grind one of the cutting surfaces smooth and then determine the shape you would like it to take. Half of the profile is ground into the end of the converted file

Scrape a rosette on the knob's face. To produce matching rosettes on multiple knobs, be sure to position the tool at the same distance from the center each time.

Decorative accents. Add a decorative element to a knob by plugging the center with a material of contrasting color.

Drill a center hole in the knob. When the knob is nearly complete, mount a drill bit in the tailstock of the lathe and slowly plunge it into the workpiece while the lathe is running.

Plug and trim the end to a finish. Experiment with different woods, materials, and designs.

along with a 10-degree angle sloping back from the cutting edge.

Once you are nearly finished turning a knob, use the custom scraper to cut the rosette pattern on its face. It's pretty hard to go wrong here; the only thing you need to be concerned with is positioning the scraper in the same location for each knob. If you hold the scraper too close to the center of the knob, the rings will have smaller diameters than a rosette cut with the scraper positioned farther away from the center.

Accent a knob with contrasting wood

Another method for decorating a knob is to add an accent with material of a contrasting color. One striking example is to use a maple plug in an ebony knob (see the photos above).

Feel free to experiment with material other than wood. In my work I've used all sorts of accents, including a ham bone right from the dinner table.

Rough out the knob's profile, leaving extra material on the end grain. Mount a ⅜-in. drill bit in the tailstock with a second Jacobs chuck. Slowly drill into the face of the knob until you've hollowed out the core to about ¼ in. deep.

Use a plug cutter the same size as the knob hole to cut the plug. (For a knob with a large diameter, the plug could be turned between centers.) Then glue the plug into the knob with epoxy. After the epoxy dries, the knob can be turned smooth and then sanded and finished.

Turn large knobs with a faceplate. Faceplate-turned knobs have the grain running across the face, which allows the grain to blend in better with the face of the drawer. This method is preferred for large-diameter knobs.

Use a faceplate to make large knobs

A spindle-turned knob is limited in its size. If it's too large, it can be problematic, because the end of the knob will drink up finish and turn the end grain much darker, which can give an unsightly appearance to the front of a piece. The best way to avoid this is to turn a cross-grain pull with a faceplate. As a result, the grain will blend much better with the face of the drawer front.

On a square block, find the centerpoint and sketch the desired diameter of the knob. Then drill a hole in the center to a depth of about ⅜ in., which will be used to mount the stock on the lathe as well as on the drawer front.

Next, prepare a faceplate for the stock. You will need a faceplate with a center screw, which is used to attach the workpiece. If you don't have a commercial screw-mounting faceplate, you can make one. Screw a piece of ¾-in.-thick plywood to a metal faceplate

Make a center-screw faceplate. Plywood screwed to a faceplate is leveled and rounded so that a wood blank can be screwed on and turned round. Drive a lag screw through the hole from behind and screw on the turning blank.

Lay out the elements of the knob. After turning the workpiece round, locate and mark with a pencil the beginning and end of the fillet, cove, and bead.

Turn the cove with a rounded scraper. The cove is asymmetrical and spans from the base diameter to the major diameter of the knob.

Round the face of the knob. Use a scraper to round over the face of the knob. Polish the shape before sanding to a finish.

and then turn the plywood round on the lathe. Then mount a drill bit in the tailstock of the lathe with a Jacobs chuck, and slowly drive the bit into the faceplate while the lathe is running. This will give you a through-hole that is centered perfectly. Next, screw a sheet-metal screw or ¼-in. lag screw into the hole from behind, effectively creating a center-screw faceplate; the screw should be sized to fit in the hole on the wood blank. The protruding end will screw into the hole drilled in the workpiece.

With the workpiece in place, cut its profile following the same steps described earlier to cut the long-grain pull. However, use scraping tools rather than spindle-turning tools because you are turning mostly end grain. Spindle tools may grab the end grain and chip or split off a chunk of the turning. I use ¼-in. square-nose, ¼-in. round-nose, and ½-in. square-nose scrapers. Mark the location of the fillet, cove, and bead with a pencil and turn them to the appropriate profile, checking for consistency with calipers along the way. Finally, sand and finish the knob, unscrew it from the faceplate, and attach it (see the facing page).

Attaching drawer knobs

Long-grain knobs. Fit the tenon through a hole on the drawer face and drive a wedge from inside (inset) into the hand-sawn kerf.

Cross-grain knobs. Use a screw with the same threading as the one used to mount the knob in the faceplate.

Authentic Shaker Knobs

CHRISTIAN BECKSVOORT

I make mostly Shaker furniture, so a number of my pieces have Shaker-style knobs—commonly called mushroom knobs—mounted to the doors and drawers. Although you can buy them, I prefer to make them. Commercial versions come in limited sizes. Plus, some of them don't quite have the graceful curves that are the hallmark of a classic Shaker knob. I'm also free to use any wood species.

Then, too, when I make my own knobs I can size them in proportion to the drawer front. For example, I make a 15-drawer chest that has 2¼-in.-tall top drawer fronts and a 5½-in.-tall bottom drawer front (see the photo at left). That piece has eight different knob sizes, varying from ⅝ in. dia. to just under ⅞ in. dia., in increments of 0.025 in., or just under 1⁄32 in.

After 30-plus years of turning these knobs, I've managed to learn a few tricks that help get the job done quickly and efficiently. In fact, I now turn a typical 1-in.-dia. knob in about eight minutes.

Early on, I realized that the tenon diameter is the only critical dimension on a knob. The tenon must fit snugly into its hole. Too big and it won't fit; too small and the joint strength is compromised. And extra glue won't correct the issue.

So rather than turn the tenons on a lathe and have to deal with some inevitable

Center the blank. Shift the base until the center of the bit is centered on the blank.

Cut the tenon. Replace the drill bit with a tenon cutter, set the depth stop at 1 in., and make the cut.

Set it free. Make a cut into all four sides. The last cut frees the outside ring.

inaccuracy, I use a drill press with a ⅜-in. or ½-in. tenon cutter (depending on the knob size) to do the work. A tenon cutter creates perfect tenons every time.

For any knob to look good, it must have correct proportions. When turning a Shaker mushroom-style knob, I make the exposed length the same as the diameter. Add about 1¼ in. to the rough blank to accommodate a 1-in. tenon and the turning process.

Make the tenon and rough-turn the blank

Begin by drawing diagonals on the end of a square blank. Mount a drill bit in a drill press and support the blank with two blocks screwed to a plywood base. Shift the base until the center of the bit is centered on the blank. Then, clamp the base to the drill-press table.

Clamp the blank to the blocks and replace the drill bit with a tenon cutter. Set the drill-press speed to 1,200 rpm for a ⅜-in. tenon cutter and 1,000 rpm for a ½-in. cutter. Set the depth stop at 1 in. and make the cut.

Measure the tenon depth and mark it on the outside of the blank. At the bandsaw, using the mark as a guide, make a cut into all four sides about ³⁄₁₆ in. deep, or as deep as you can go without cutting into the tenon. The last cut frees the outside ring.

Slip the tenon into a three-jawed chuck, leaving about ¼ in. of the tenon exposed. Set a caliper to the desired knob diameter, and then use a gouge to turn the blank from square to round. Check your progress frequently. You've arrived at the correct size when the caliper just clears the turning.

To turn the shoulder use the same caliper setting to mark the knob length, measuring from the front of the blank. Use a parting tool or a beading-and-parting tool to undercut the base of the knob by a few degrees.

Rough in the outside. Use a gouge to turn the blank from square to round (left). Check your progress frequently. You've arrived at the correct size when the caliper just clears the turning (right).

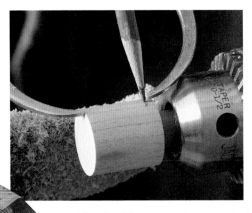

Turn the shoulder. Measuring from the front of the blank, use the same caliper setting to mark the knob length (left). Undercut the base of the knob by a few degrees with a parting tool or a beading-and-parting tool (right).

Mark the rim. Mark the location of the outside rim of the knob about ¼ in. from the end.

Begin to turn the stem. Using a small gouge, start to turn the profile behind the rim of the knob.

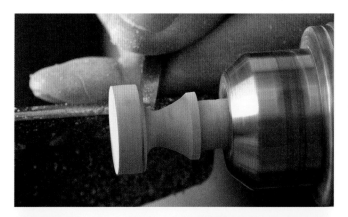

Shape the cap. Use the small round-nose scraper to turn the flared cap on the end of the knob.

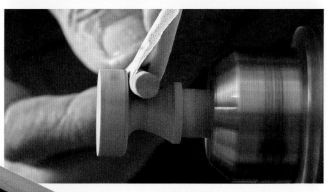

How to tame a tricky area. To shape the tight curve behind the rim use a small round-nose scraper (top). When close to the desired shape, use sandpaper wrapped around a dowel to make a smooth radius (above).

Sand the knob. With the knob spinning, start sanding (top). Avoid rounding the edge of the cap (above).

Turn the curves

With a pencil, mark the location of the outside rim of the knob about ¼ in. from the end (see the bottom left photo, facing page). Using a small gouge, start to turn the profile behind the rim of the knob.

Use a small round-nose scraper to shape the tight curve behind the rim. Once close to the desired shape, use sandpaper wrapped around a dowel to make a smooth radius.

The small round-nose scraper is used once again, this time to turn the flared cap on the end of the knob. Avoid reducing the diameter at the rim of the cap. With the knob spinning, start sanding with P150-grit paper, then P220-grit. Avoid rounding the edge of the cap. Polish the cap with 0000 steel wool.

Cut the tenon to final length

The knob can spin out of your hands if cut freehand on the bandsaw. The cut will be safer and easier if you make a little carriage. It also makes it easier to get a square cut. To make the jig, drill a hole for the knob's tenon in a piece of stock. Then saw that piece in half as shown in the top photos on p. 108.

A helpful jig. It's safer and easier to cut the tenon if you make a little carriage. If cut freehand, the knob can spin out of your hands.

Trouble-free trimming. The jig secures the tenon, allowing the knob to clear the bandsaw table.

Place the tenon in the carriage with the shoulder butting against the jig. The jig secures the tenon, holding it level while allowing the knob to clear the bandsaw table.

Attach the knob

If damp weather causes the tenon to swell, it can be made to fit without much fuss. Slip the tenon into any vise and squeeze. Repeat, turning the knob slightly each time until the entire circumference of the tenon has been slightly compressed. Once glue is added, the compressed wood will swell, creating a super-tight fit that's sure to hold fast.

Tenon too big? If damp weather causes the tenon to swell, it can be made to fit. Slip the tenon into any vise and squeeze. Repeat, turning the knob slightly each time.

Handle with care. Rather than attach a knob by tapping it with a mallet or hammer, which can dent, deform, or even break it, squeeze the knob into place using a hand screw with a strip of leather taped to the jaws.

Pens Make Great Gifts

BARRY GROSS

More furniture makers should try turning a pen. You already have most of the tools you need, you probably have the wood, and if you've done any wood turning at all, you have the skills.

Not only is pen turning fun, but pens also make great gifts, both for the recipient and for the maker. In the time you'd spend making a box—never mind a small piece of furniture—you can make half a dozen pens and get six heartfelt thank-yous instead of one.

Pen turning can be done on any lathe with a few specialized tools. I'll tell you which of these tools are essential and which ones can be duplicated by tools you probably already own. I'll tell you what pen hardware to buy, what woods work well, how to turn and finish the blanks, and, last, how to assemble the pen.

Preparing the pen blank

Woodworkers often ask me what wood makes the best pen and I half-jokingly reply any wood they rejected for furniture making. Examples include gnarly or crotch sections of boards, isolated patches of figure or curl, or even pieces of firewood with spalting in it. Remember, you want a blank that is less than 1 in. square by 5 in. long. For this reason, burls are a good choice because their tight, swirly grain pattern is the right scale. If the scrap bin or the firewood pile is exhausted, one of the benefits of wood turning is the opportunity to try new and exotic species such as amboyna burl, lignum vitae, or red palm for $2 to $8 a blank. You can also buy eye-catching composite woods and acrylic blanks.

Once you've selected the pen kit and the material for the body, you can get started. Depending on whether your kit has a one-part or two-part body (or barrel), place the pen tube(s) on the pen blank and mark it for length, adding 1/16 in. to each end. Label the sections and then cut the parts to length.

What makes a pen different from a typical spindle turning is the long hole through the center, and the metal tube(s) you glue into it. You can drill the pen blank on the drill press or on the lathe. For the former you'll need to clamp the blank and ensure it is in line with the drill bit. On the lathe, a dedicated pen-drilling chuck is the easiest way to center the blank to the drill bit, but you also can hold the workpiece in a four-jaw chuck.

Once the pen blanks have been drilled, glue the tubes into them. Roughen the outside

Tools of the trade

THREE TURNING TOOLS

Full-size tools suitable for turning a table leg are too big for delicate pen turning. Medium-size or small tools are more responsive. The good news is that you only need three.

1. **⁵⁄₁₆-in. to ½-in. roughing gouge** Used to turn the square blank down to a round.
2. **½-in. skew chisel** Used to profile the blank, smooth the cylinder, and bring the ends almost flush with the bushings.

or

2a. **½-in. Spindlemaster** Designed to leave a smooth finish like the skew chisel without the risk of catching. Use instead of the skew.
3. **⅛-in. parting tool** Used to remove finish from the bushings and to achieve a clean break with the blanks.

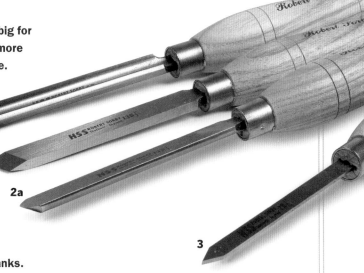

BARREL TRIMMER

This tool ensures that the turned blanks will fit together seamlessly with the parts of the pen kit. Attached to a drill, the shaft removes any excess glue from inside the tube and also aligns the cutter as it trims the end of the blank flush with the end of the tube.

Barrel trimmer

GLUE AND ABRASIVE PADS

Super Glue creates a very durable finish. Special sanding pads bring it to a high shine.

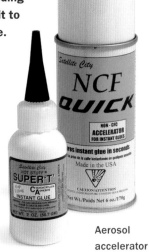

Aerosol accelerator

Cyanoacrylate glue

PEN MANDREL

A mandrel supports the blanks while you turn them on the lathe. Most come with a 7-mm drill bit and a set of 7-mm bushings that match the standard pen kit. The step bushings indicate the diameter to which the blanks must be turned.

Mandrel

7-mm drill bit

Bushings

Abrasive pads

Buyer's guide to pen hardware

All pens require a kit of metal parts. Choices include ball point, roller ball, or fountain; a pen that twists or clicks open; or one with a single or a double barrel. The typical ball-point kit consists of one or two brass tubes that you place inside the drilled-out pen blanks, a top clip and cap assembly, a twist or click mechanism, a refill, and a bottom or nib section. I'd start with a "cigar-style" kit (shown below). It gives a good introduction to wood selection, turning, and finishing. Avoid 24-karat and 10-karat gold plating, which wears off quickly to expose the brass inside. Titanium nitride (TN) gold plating is better. Even more durable is chrome or black chrome, but I prefer rhodium (sometimes misnamed platinum). It lasts essentially forever.

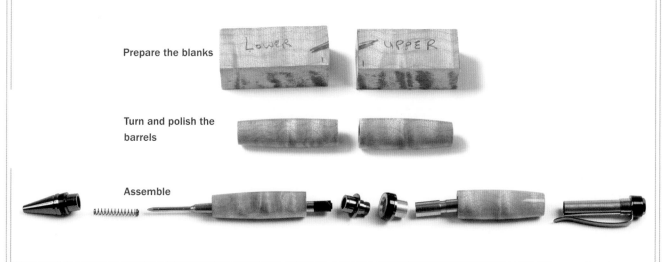

Prepare the blanks

Turn and polish the barrels

Assemble

of the pen tubes with 80-grit sandpaper. I also size natural or unstabilized wood by dripping some thin cyanoacrylate glue down the holes. Both actions give the glue for the tubes a better surface to bond to. When it is dry, place some medium-thick cyanoacrylate glue or five-minute epoxy on a piece of glossy paper or plastic, roll a tube in it, and then use a specialized insertion tool or a nail punch to hold the pen tubes so you do not get glue all over your fingers. Push the tubes into the blanks until they are about 1/16 in. inside each end. You'll bring the ends flush to the tubes later when trimming them clean and square. You can do this before or after rough-turning the blank using either a barrel trimmer in a handheld drill or a squaring jig and a disk sander equipped with a miter gauge. Take

off the excess slowly until you just reach the brass tube.

Turning and finishing the blanks

To secure the pen blank while you turn and finish it, you use a mandrel, which goes into those tubes you inserted earlier. Hold the mandrel in the head stock of the lathe via a Morse taper or an attachment to a chuck, and place the step bushings and prepared pen blanks on the mandrel following the instructions in the pen kit. Do not overtighten the nut on the mandrel because this will cause the mandrel to bow slightly and you'll turn the blanks out of round. I prefer to turn one pen blank at a time to reduce the chances of vibration.

Prepare the pen blanks. Before you turn the blanks, you need to drill them and insert the brass tubes that come with the pen kit. Start by laying out the blank. Each section should be a little over ⅛ in. longer than its respective tube. Label the parts and mark their relationship for grain continuity.

Drilling on the lathe is easiest. Cut the parts to length, then secure each blank in a pen-drilling chuck or a conventional four-jaw chuck (shown).

Stabilize the blanks. In any natural wood (as opposed to impregnated or stabilized woods sold for pen turning), you should "size" the holes with thin cyanoacrylate glue.

Rough up the tubes. Rub the pen tubes on 80-grit sandpaper to give them better adhesion when you glue them into the blanks.

Work fast. Spread medium-viscosity cyanoacrylate glue on some glossy paper. Roll a tube in the glue and then use either a dedicated insertion tool or a nail punch to push it into the blank.

Square up the ends. To bring the ends of the blank flush with the ends of the tubes, you can use a barrel trimmer mounted in a handheld drill as shown, or a miter gauge on a disk sander.

With the lathe speed set at approximately 2,000 rpm, start with a roughing gouge to get the blank round. Next, use a skew and turn the blank down to the step bushings, adding a little shape to the blank if desired. If you are skew "challenged," use a Spindlemaster. This tool is a beginner's best friend because it does not have the sharp points of a skew to catch and dig in, and it leaves almost as good a finish.

For the last pass, use the skew or the Spindlemaster as a scraper to lightly pass over the blank and bring the ends almost flush with the bushings. Start sanding with P180-grit or P220-grit sandpaper and work your way up to 800-grit. To remove the microscopic scratches that sandpaper will leave, I give the blanks a very brief touchup with 500-grit, 1,000-grit, 2,000-grit, and 4,000-grit Abralon sanding pads.

Super Glue is the pen-turner's secret finish

A high-gloss finish best displays the wood's beauty, but because of the frequent handling that pens get, it needs to be durable. You can use solvent-based lacquer, but the most durable shine comes from cyanoacrylate glue, which is in fact a type of acrylic. With the lathe turning at around 150 rpm and wearing disposable gloves, dribble some medium-thick cyanoacrylate glue onto the blank while holding a paper towel against the underside (see the top photos on p. 114). Thin glue wicks into the towel too fast and will not apply evenly.

Apply the glue by moving the towel back and forth as the pen blank is turning. Keep moving the towel so it does not stick to the pen blank, then spray on some accelerator to dry the glue quickly, and apply three more coats in the same way. Don't worry about getting glue on the bushings; you'll remove it later.

Once you've applied four coats, turn off the lathe and sand parallel to the lathe with 320-grit sandpaper to remove any ridges. Turn the lathe back on at 2,000 rpm and, with a small parting tool, remove the glue on the bushings close to the pen blank. This will make it easier to remove the bushings from the pen blank later.

Wet-sanding and polishing

With the finish smooth, you can use acrylic sanding pads to polish it. The six grits range from 600-grit up to 12,000-grit and are color-coded by grit. Place a towel on the lathe bed to protect it and wet a 600-grit pad with water. Use a medium amount of pressure and wet-sand for about 10 seconds per pen blank. Wipe off the resulting white slurry, move on to the next grit, and repeat the process.

Remove the pen blanks from the mandrel. If a blank is stuck to the bushings, lightly tap it on the lathe to break the bond. Your

Round it. Insert the correct size bushing (above). Use a roughing gouge to turn the square blank round (right).

Refine it. Use a Spindlemaster (left), or if you are comfortable with it, a skew chisel to bring the blank to its final size and shape. To bring the ends of the blank flush with the bushings, use the skew (right) or Spindlemaster like a scraper.

Sand it. Smooth the wood with sandpaper to 800-grit, then switch to Abralon cushioned abrasive pads and go up to 4,000-grit.

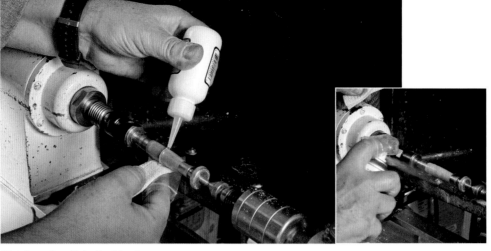

Finish and polish the blanks. Apply medium-thick cyanoacrylate glue to the turning blank as you spread it with a paper towel. Wear a disposable glove or wrap your finger in a plastic bag. Use an aerosol accelerator to instantly cure the cyanoacrylate finish (inset photo).

Smooth the finish. After four coats of finish are applied, use 320-grit paper to remove any ridges.

Unstick the blank. Use a parting tool to scrape off any glue from the bushings.

Polish the finish. Use a series of increasingly fine abrasive pads designed for acrylic to polish the finish.

Assemble the pen. You can buy a pen press to assemble the pen, but as long as you protect the components, a metalworking (or woodworking) vise works almost as well.

blanks will almost certainly have a higher sheen than anything else you've made, but if tiny scratches are still visible, you can buff them off. Hold the pen blanks perpendicular to a buffing wheel treated with a compound (in this case a blue acrylic polish), and apply a bit of pressure. Then polish the blanks on a cotton flannel wheel to bring up the ultimate shine.

Line up the pen parts according to the instructions in the kit. Use a pen press, drill press, or bench vise to apply light pressure to press (not glue) the pieces into the pen blanks. Use scraps of wood to avoid any metal-to-metal contact that might damage the pen components. Congratulations, you've just finished what I'm sure will be the first of many pens.

Get a Handle on Your Chisels

BOB SMALSER

Have some old socket chisels around that need handles? If not, perhaps you should. Even with today's high collector interest, flea markets, estate sales, and auctions still provide excellent values in tools if you can make your own handles. I prefer my own handles anyway, as I custom-fit them to the size of my hands and to my working style.

What's the big deal about old socket chisels in the first place? They generally are premium tools, made when chisels were drop-forged instead of investment-cast. Except for price (a handleless old chisel often can be had for less than $5), the differences between an old Thomas Witherby or James Swan and a modern chisel are subtle, but many of my generation still consider them to be the best compromise between edge retention and ease of sharpening

Shape the handle. Start by turning a stub tenon. The author uses a parting tool to form the tenon, and then glues leather washers over it to create a durable striking surface.

Establish the tenon shoulder. Use the parting tool to mark the start of tenon that fits in the chisel socket, then shape the adjacent tapered section with a small gouge.

Cut the handle to final shape. Use the small gouge followed by a skew chisel for cleanup. This design relies on subtle curves for comfort.

Handle dimensions

After turning more than a hundred handles for himself and tradesmen friends, Smalser finds these dimensions most comfortable for a man with large hands.

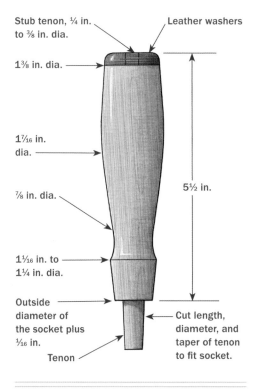

Stub tenon, ¼ in. to ⅜ in. dia.

Leather washers

1⅜ in. dia.

1⁷⁄₁₆ in. dia.

⅞ in. dia.

5½ in.

1¹⁄₁₆ in. to 1¼ in. dia.

Outside diameter of the socket plus ¹⁄₁₆ in.

Tenon

Cut length, diameter, and taper of tenon to fit socket.

Shape the tenon. Use an inside-outside caliper. Transfer the inside diameter of the socket mouth to the tenon shoulder, checking progress as you cut the top of the tenon to size with a parting tool.

Finish the taper. Gauge the socket's depth and its diameter at the deep end. Use these measurements, and the parting tool, to cut the small end of the tenon to size. Finish the taper by pulling a small skew from the tenon shoulder to the pointed end. Leave the tenon slightly oversize for hand-fitting later.

Sand and finish the handle. Begin sanding with 120-grit. Work through the grits up to 320-grit.

Raise the grain. Wipe the handle with a damp towel between each grit. The water swells and loosens the wood fibers in the scratches, so less work is required to sand them off.

Apply the finish. The author prefers a thin wiping varnish formulated for gunstocks (Tru-Oil® or Lin-Speed®), rubbed out with paste wax and #0000 steel wool after curing.

in a factory-made chisel. They also are relatively plentiful—there were a couple dozen premium chisel manufacturers in the decades before World War II, not just the two or three best known. I like to see those heritage tools in the hands of users instead of collecting dust.

To make a good handle, any dense hardwood will do. Use what you have locally so you can make matching handles later. The original factories used common woods like hickory, ash, and oak pretty interchangeably. I suppose the hardest, toughest, and heaviest woods with interlocked grain are best— woods like dogwood and hop hornbeam— but I haven't found one species to outlast another in normal use. A teenager with a framing hammer can destroy any one of them as easily as another.

An age-old fitting trick. After securing the blade in a vise, insert the tenon firmly and twist it a full revolution. A dirty socket will leave dark patches on the high spots; file these away using a fine rasp. Repeat until you have full wood-to-metal contact for a perfect fit.

Drive the socket tenon home with a mallet.
Leave a gap between the socket and the tenon
shoulder. This helps prevent splitting. You also
can seat the tenon and shoulder in epoxy to
prevent the handle from coming loose when the
handle shrinks in the dry season.

Here in the hardwood-scarce Northwest,
I use Pacific madrone, simply because it's
the densest of the three hardwood species
growing in my woods.

I use a lathe, but you can make handles
without one. Anything done on a lathe
can be done as well, just not as fast, using a
drawknife, a spokeshave, rasps, and files.

Fixing a tenon that's too small

A tenon that's too skinny
won't fit securely. Simply
cut a piece of cloth to fit
the tenon's length and
circumference, wrap it
around the tenon, and glue it
in place as a shim. Once the
glue dries, drive the handle
into the socket.

Turn a Hollow Vessel

HOWARD LEWIN

During the past few decades there has been a revolution in wood-turning tools, from lathes and chucks to gouges and boring bars. As a result, what once was deemed difficult or even impossible to turn has become commonplace.

In the area of hollow-vessel turning, two innovators stand out. The first is David Ellsworth, who in the 1970s began turning vessels with small openings. His first tools were scrapers he had bent with a welding torch. Later he developed longer-handled tools with swivel tips that held machinist's tool bits. These offered more control and

safety and could produce a wider variety of enclosed-vessel forms. Jerry Glaser, an aerospace engineer and hobbyist wood turner, took the ball from there, working to reduce the long tool's tendency to catch and jerk downward. He came up with a double-articulating tip that swivels to place the cutting edge at the tool's centerline. Other variations continue to emerge, making new vessel forms possible.

I use a Glaser-designed boring bar for my hollow-vessel work. The tool is available from the *Woodturners Catalog* (www.woodturnerscatalog.com). The bar is

High-tech hollowing tool. Lewin uses a boring bar, which has a counterweight and a double-articulating tip that keeps the cutting edge on the centerline of the tool. It is designed to prevent violent catches, the biggest problem in hollowing.

Shape the outside first

Turn the outside of this piece just as you would the outside of any green-wood vessel. Start by locating the blank in a log and chainsawing it free. Remember, in this end-grain vessel, the grain runs straight through the piece from top to bottom (see the drawing on the facing page). You can choose a face-grain blank with the grain running from side to side through the piece, but the end-grain orientation is a bit more stable during the hollowing and drying processes.

Rough out the general shape on the bandsaw, cutting the bottom of the blank as flat as possible for a good mounting surface. Attach the faceplate with at least six or eight #8 by 1½-in. coarse-threaded drywall screws. After mounting the long blank on the lathe, put a live center in the tailstock and tighten it against the far end.

It helps immensely to have a variable-speed lathe, because a large blank must revolve slowly at first to create an appropriate cutting speed at the outer edges. Then, as the workpiece gets smaller, the lathe speed can be increased slowly to create the same ideal cutting speed at the perimeter. However, if you have a finite number of speeds to choose from, err on the side of caution. It's better to take a little more time than risk a flying workpiece.

I turn the outside using a long, hefty bowl gouge developed by Glaser, which is also available from the *Woodturners Catalog*. The tool, which features A-11 tool steel, a deep flute, and an extreme fingernail profile on the tip, makes the task go quickly and smoothly (see the photos on the facing page). With the grain running parallel to the bed of the lathe, all cutting on the outside should be done downhill—as if it were a spindle turning. In other words, cut from the largest diameter toward the narrowest areas. The last pass, a

filled with buckshot to dampen vibration. The tip is double-articulated, and a large counterweight attached to the bar reduces the impact of catches, which can be murder on the wrists. This tool's innovative design makes cutting into end grain much less daunting. The other key to success is using green wood.

Aside from the joy and ease of turning wet wood—ribbons just stream off the workpiece, even in end grain—I also like the subtle way green wood moves and dries. Many turners avoid green wood because of its tendency to crack as it dries. However, the drying process is easily controlled, reducing the likelihood of checking. The first key is to keep the vessel walls thin and uniform, which not only allow the walls to flex but also equalize drying stresses. The second is to wrap the freshly turned vessel in brown paper bags to slow the release of moisture. Following these guidelines, I seldom see checks or cracks.

A shape emerges

Orienting the blank with the grain, not across it, makes the green-wood vessel more stable during the drying process. Avoid the unstable center of the log for the same reason.

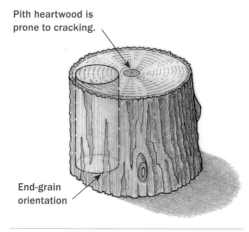

Pith heartwood is prone to cracking.

End-grain orientation

Don't fight the grain. With the grain running parallel to the bed of the lathe, all cuts should be made from high areas to low areas. The blank is mounted on a faceplate, with the tailstock (and a live center) engaged to steady the blank.

light planing cut with the gouge riding its bevel, leaves a smooth surface.

I like to turn a shallow foot at the bottom of my vessels, roughly one-third of the vessel's diameter and long enough to contain the screw holes. Later, after hollowing the inside of the vessel, I'll hollow the foot as well, which will remove the screw holes and keep the walls of the vessel roughly ¼ in. thick for successful drying.

Hollow out the inside

After sliding the tailstock out of the way, drill a hole to establish the depth of the cavity and to give the boring bar a place to start. You can put the bit in a drill chuck and hold the chuck in your hands to drill the hole. Just support the bit on a tool rest as you feed it into the center of the stock. As the hole nears its final depth, check it frequently against the overall height of the vessel. Be sure to figure in the height of the foot and thickness of the bottom wall.

The 3/16-in.-square tool bit on the Glaser boring bar can either scrape the wood or

The last pass is a planing cut. Turn the gouge and rest the bevel against the workpiece. For a smooth cut, gently pivot the tool until it begins cutting, and keep the bevel in contact with the stock.

Bowl gouge

An extreme fingernail grind gets the corners out of the way. The gouge can be angled sharply in each direction to make planing cuts on convex and concave surfaces.

Hollowing, step by step

After drilling an entrance hole, plunge the boring bar from the center out to the inner wall of the vessel to make each cut. You'll need to readjust the articulated tip of the tool as you work your way deeper into the vessel.

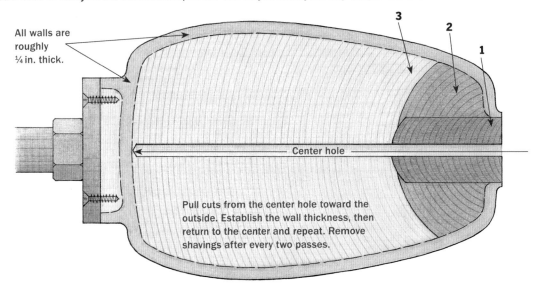

All walls are roughly ¼ in. thick.

3 **2** **1**

Center hole

Pull cuts from the center hole toward the outside. Establish the wall thickness, then return to the center and repeat. Remove shavings after every two passes.

1. MAKE SOME ROOM TO WORK

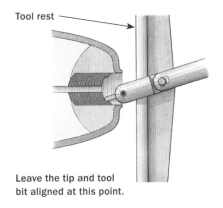

Tool rest

Leave the tip and tool bit aligned at this point.

2. REACH AROUND THE CORNER

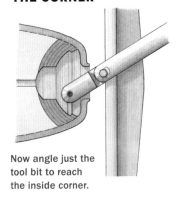

Now angle just the tool bit to reach the inside corner.

3. COMPLETE THE HOLLOWING

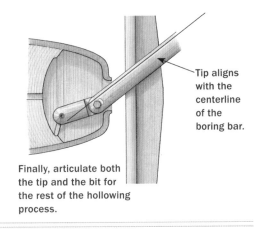

Tip aligns with the centerline of the boring bar.

Finally, articulate both the tip and the bit for the rest of the hollowing process.

slice it, depending on the angle at which it's held. Scraping is not usually feasible with green wood, but this small bit resists catches, which happen when the tool gets stuck in the wood, often drawing it in more deeply and damaging the workpiece. The angle I favor for hollowing is halfway between the two—sort of a peel. The mass of the boring bar and counterweight keep it steady. The tool bit is cobalt high-speed steel and will hold an edge for a long time.

After the hole has been drilled, set the double-articulated tip of the boring bar in a straight line (see the drawings above) and begin to widen the opening to give yourself enough room to work. Then articulate the end into the hook shape to reach around the inside corner. As soon as possible, realign the tip of the tool bit with the centerline of the bar to reduce the torque on your wrists.

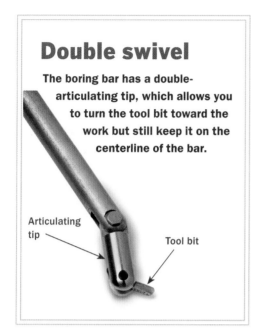

Double swivel

The boring bar has a double-articulating tip, which allows you to turn the tool bit toward the work but still keep it on the centerline of the bar.

Articulating tip

Tool bit

Drill a deep hole to establish the final depth. Lewin uses a long drill in a handheld chuck, supporting the bit on a tool rest. He pauses every 1 in. or so to clear chips, and he checks the depth frequently near the bottom.

The diameter of the entrance hole is an important design consideration. Many turners try to keep this opening very small to demonstrate their skills and to confound collectors. I don't go to those extremes, but I like to keep the hole small enough to be pleasing to the eye and keep probing fingers and eyes from the interior. That way I don't have to attempt to sand the inside.

Open the entrance. This is done with the articulating tip of a boring bar set in a straight position.

Cut from the center out

The order and direction of the cuts when hollowing is the same for any end-grain vessel, open or closed; it's just a little more painstaking and time-consuming with the boring bar and the small tool bit than it is with a bowl gouge. Each cut starts at the center and is pulled toward the inner wall of the vessel. Green wood is especially pliable, so once a thin wall has been established, it becomes too floppy to return to later. So work toward the wall, establish the right thickness and then move back to the center of the hollowed area to begin another cut. Don't attempt to take a little off an area that you turned five passes earlier. There won't be enough material

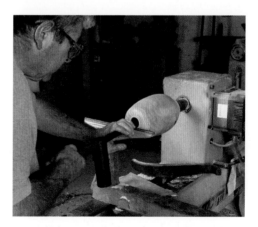

Then swivel the tip and begin hollowing. All cuts in this end-grain vessel start at the center hole and are pulled toward the inner wall of the vessel.

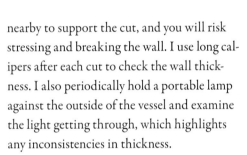

Finish the foot. Reverse-mount the vessel to hollow the foot. Use a jam chuck (above) and a cup center (left). The cup center is less likely to split the bottom of the vessel than a live center.

Use a thin gouge to work around the center. Hollowing the foot removes the screw holes and leaves the walls and bottom the same thickness as the rest of the vessel, which is important to the drying process.

nearby to support the cut, and you will risk stressing and breaking the wall. I use long calipers after each cut to check the wall thickness. I also periodically hold a portable lamp against the outside of the vessel and examine the light getting through, which highlights any inconsistencies in thickness.

You must remove shavings from the inside as you go. Centrifugal force will plaster them against the side of the vessel, making the surface very difficult to penetrate. Trying to force the tool through this layer generally ends in disaster because the tool catches and goes through the side. I stop the lathe every two passes and use compressed air and a shop vacuum to clean out the vessel.

When you reach the bottom of the drilled hole, the hollowing is done. Check the bottom thickness with the lamp just as you did the sides.

Leave the vessel on the faceplate for about a day to let the surface moisture flash off, then remount it on the lathe and sand the outside.

The finished piece. One last sanding after it's dry, a few coats of lacquer, and the vessel is ready for display.

Hollow the foot and dry the vessel

Last, remove the vessel from the faceplate, mount it in the reverse position, and hollow out the foot so all the walls are the same thickness. The reverse position is achieved with a jam chuck and a live center with a cup-shaped tip. The cup center is much less likely to split the bottom than a pointed center.

I do this hollowing with a thin bowl gouge, which allows me to work around the live center. The small tenon left connecting the vessel to the center can be knocked off later with a sharp chisel.

Now the vessel is ready for final drying. With three or four paper bags wrapped around it and curled shut, the vessel should be able to relieve its own stresses as it slowly releases moisture. Be ready for some subtle warps or bulges as the vessel goes from wet to dry. I think of these mysterious changes as the character of the tree revealing itself.

When the bags feel dry to the touch— usually after 5 to 10 days—the piece is dry. Give it a fine sanding by hand and seal it with your finish of choice.

Turning Bowls from Green Wood

HOWARD LEWIN

I've heard it too many times, even from expert wood turners: Don't bother with green wood. Sure, it's wonderful to turn, but the bowls always crack. Well, they're wrong. It is possible to turn and dry green bowls successfully, and you won't need any polyethylene glycol (PEG), complicated procedures, or other hocus-pocus to do it. There are just a few techniques to be mastered and a couple of tricks to be learned. Soon your success rate will make green wood fun and worthwhile.

The lure of turning green wood has always been strong. I can think of at least six good reasons why you should try it. First, freshly downed logs are often free. This lets you experiment and grow as a turner without worrying about cost. I live in Los Angeles, where tree trimmers have to pay to dump their loads. I let them dump wood at my studio. They grind up the small branches and sell that as mulch. I keep the logs, freshly cut and delivered free. Even if you can't swing a deal like mine, you can probably meet your local tree trimmer on site and take some logs away. Less work for him.

Second, the selection of green wood is almost unlimited. Wherever you live, a variety of species is available to turners who keep their eyes and ears open. Third, you're not limited in size to what's in the lumberyard. Ask your local lumber salesman for a 12-in. by 12-in. by 12-in. walnut bowl blank. You'll get a blank look.

Fourth, turning green wood is more pleasant. New wood is softer, making the cutting easier and faster. Tools stay cooler, keeping them sharper longer. Green wood produces less dust and creates larger shavings, which are easier to pick up. Green bowls can be wet-sanded, which creates no dust at all. And green wood is easier to cut with chainsaws and bandsaws. Shall I go on?

A fifth reason to turn green stock is that it allows total freedom. Because the wood is soft and cuts easily, bowls and vessels can be shaped with very thin walls. End-grain vessel shapes become not only possible but also easy. One of my favorite shapes includes the bark and the center of the log, with heartwood bull's-eyes on the sides. These forms are very difficult to achieve with dry wood. Also, when the wood dries, the pith sometimes bulges out in an interesting way. And that's the sixth benefit: The final shape of the vessel is often undetermined. Once the piece has been set aside to dry, mystical changes take place. I have had bowls almost close and others twist like a pretzel, all

without cracking. And there are tricks for manipulating the final shape in strange ways.

Getting started

Now you know why you should try green wood, but you need to understand how. It starts with a chainsaw; I recommend having two. Use a gas-powered one for felling and cutting up trees, and get an electric one for use in your shop. There's no exhaust, and it's easier on your ears (and your neighbors) on a leisurely Sunday morning.

Watch out for nails in wood that was in a yard or near a road, and cut logs about 6 in.

Six reasons for turning green wood

1. **Fresh logs are often free.**

2. **There's a wide selection of species.**

3. **Large blanks are easy to come by.**

4. **It cuts fast with little dust.**

5. **It's easy to turn thin walls and unconventional shapes.**

6. **Final shape changes during drying.**

Locating bowl blanks within the log

Designing green-wood vessels starts with seeing the potential blank locations in each log. For this chapter three types of bowls were turned from a length of ficus. Bowls 1 and 2 are face-grain vessels. However, Bowl 1's upper edge is oriented toward the center of the log, with some of the pith captured in the rim, whereas Bowl 2 is a natural-edged vessel, with its rim defined by the outside of the log. Bowl 3 is an end-grain vessel. For stability, it is located away from the pith heartwood, the 2-in. or 3-in. core of heartwood that is the densest area of the log and the most prone to moving and checking during drying.

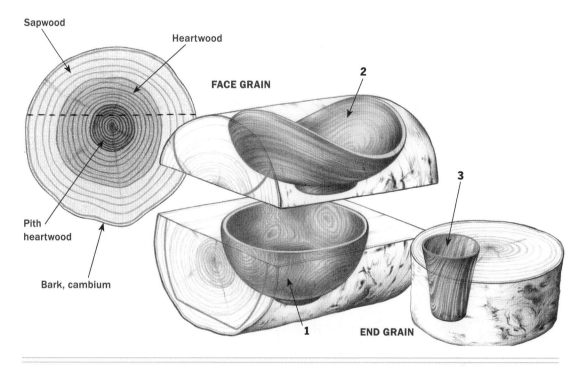

Sapwood

Heartwood

FACE GRAIN

2

Pith heartwood

Bark, cambium

3

1

END GRAIN

longer than you need, to allow for checking. Most beginners run into trouble cutting the log down the middle. This is an important cut in preparing green wood for turning, because many bowl forms are made from log halves or quarters. Also, it lets you get at the center of the log if you plan to remove the middle 2 in. or 3 in., which contains the pith and the densest heartwood. This pith heartwood, as I call it, is the area most likely to split, so its removal will help prevent checking if a blank must be stored for a while.

When cutting a log lengthwise, the temptation is to set it on end and cut down. This is slow going because you are cutting into end grain the entire length of the log. Lay down the log and cut parallel to its

length. You'll get longer shavings and a faster cut. To prevent dangerous kickback, never tilt the chainsaw bar forward while its tip is engaged in the wood. Clear the long shavings often so they don't bind the chain. And be sure to prop the log so that it won't roll. When you're almost through the log, roll it over or set it on end to finish the cut.

Don't cut the wood into blanks until you need them. Work from one end of the log, and keep the ends of the log sealed with wax or paint. Don't expect a log to stay check-free for more than a few months, depending on local heat and humidity.

Use a bandsaw to cut log halves into blanks. Don't overload your machine. If you can afford it, you'll need a bandsaw that can

Chainsaw releases blanks from logs

The first step in turning a green bowl is chainsawing. A 16-in. bar is big enough for most work yet easy to handle. The author uses a gas-powered chainsaw outdoors and an electric one inside. As always when chainsawing, beware of kickback when the tip of the bar is buried in the wood.

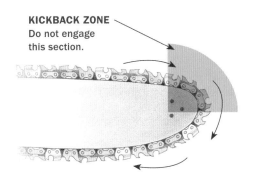

KICKBACK ZONE
Do not engage this section.

Crosscutting. The first slice gets rid of small checks at the end of the log. Any cracks must be eliminated, or they will grow later during drying.

Use a marker to plan your bowl-blank locations. This ficus log will yield two face-grain bowls, one with the pith heartwood near its rim, and the other with natural (bark) edges. Ficus, known commonly as a narrow tree used for interior decoration, grows quite large in warm climates.

The next crosscut establishes the length of the blank. Be sure to raise the log off the ground slightly to protect the saw teeth, and wedge it to prevent rolling.

Cutting lengthwise. Lay the log on its side. Placing the log on its end to make the cut (inset) means you'll be cutting into end grain the entire way. The sawdust will be fine, and the going slow. Cutting the log on its side will be much easier. Clear the long shavings often by lifting the saw out of the cut. When the saw's tip is buried in the wood, never tilt the bar forward or dangerous kickback will result.

cut about 12 in. high with a 20-in. throat and a 2-hp motor. Most of what you turn will fit into this dimensional range. Use a skip-tooth blade with about three or four teeth per inch. A hook-tooth blade will not shed wet sawdust well. I use an old tablesaw blade to mark an outline on the blank. Then I cut away as much of the unnecessary wood as possible.

Choosing blanks

A word here on locating bowl blanks in the log. With face-grain bowls, there is going to be some distortion during the drying process no matter what you do. However, the farther away from the pith heartwood, the less a face-grain bowl will move. With end-grain bowls and vase forms, there's very little movement, especially in wood away from the center. Personally, I like to include the pith heartwood in the bowl. The subsequent movement adds mystery to the final piece. I often mount the pith-heartwood side on the faceplate and turn natural-edged bowls so that the heartwood and its color are in the bottom and wall of the bowl.

Seal the end grain of green turning blanks and keep them out of the sun. But don't put them in plastic bags. They will begin to rot, and you'll never get that odor out of the wood. If you want spalting, set one end of the log on soil and wait a few months. Leave it there too long, and you'll get complete dry rot.

Mounting techniques

Three- and four-jaw chucks and expansion chucks tend to crush green wood. A screw chuck (simply a heavy wood screw protruding from a flat plate) is a viable alternative, but the bottom of the blank must be very flat to snug up against the plate. Also, green wood provides weaker threads than dry wood for this type of chuck. However, a bit of cyanoacrylate glue in the screw hole will add some holding power.

The best and safest mounting device is the faceplate. For most bowls, a 3-in. plate is sufficient. There should be at least six screw holes, large enough for #10 screws. I use 1-in. or 1¼-in. drywall screws with coarse threads for most bowls; they work great. Generally, use longer screws for end grain, because the threads don't grab as well there. And it's a good idea to flatten the blank's mounting surface.

A few general tips on turning bowls: A variable-speed lathe is great because it lets you gradually adjust the speed right up to the point before the lathe begins to vibrate. Adjust the speed and the tool rest often, keeping the leverage point as close to the work as possible. An excellent safety precaution is to keep the lathe's drive belts

Bandsawing the blanks. After chainsawing the log, the bandsaw is your next stop. Remove as much waste as possible while keeping the blank somewhat balanced. A large bandsaw and a massive lathe are nice to have, but smaller equipment just means smaller vessels.

Bowl 1 comes from the larger face-grain blank. First, a flat is cut for mounting the faceplate. The author uses a sawblade to trace the outline of the bowl onto the blank, and the waste is cut away.

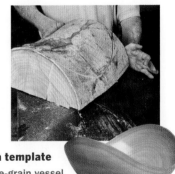

The sawblade also serves as a template for Bowl 2, a natural-edged, face-grain vessel. Again a marker transfers the bowl shape to the bark, and the waste is cut away.

The blank for Bowl 3, an end-grain vessel, is cut from another chunk of ficus. Trim away as much waste as possible.

loose enough that they will slip when the gouge gets caught in the work. This has prevented many disasters in my shop.

Turning the outside

Slide the tailstock and live center up against the blank for added holding power while roughing and shaping the outside of the bowl. Use long, hefty bowl gouges as opposed to scrapers, which will cause tearout. Examine the wood carefully for any checks or cracking. All checks must be completely turned out, or they will grow later.

When cutting on the inside or outside, choose the direction of your cut carefully. Avoid cutting against the grain, which will cause tearout and grab the tool.

Thin, even wall is the key

Once the outside of the bowl has been shaped, slide the tailstock away and begin the hollowing process. Turn the bowl to a uniform wall thickness of ¼ in. to ½ in.—thinnest for harder woods, which move more. To gauge wall thickness as you work, check the light passing through the wall of the bowl and listen to the tool resonate on the wood. The uniform thickness of the wall and bottom is one of the keys to success with green wood. As the bowl dries, it will do so evenly. Another key element is the thin wall. With most of the mass gone, the wood can relieve stress by moving freely rather than cracking. Whatever the thickness, however, it must be consistent throughout the vessel.

Once you begin hollowing, speed is of the essence. The bowl will start changing shape as it gets thinner and begins to shed water. This is no time for a break. With practice you will be able to turn a 12-in. bowl in 30 minutes. Start by plunging about 1 in. to 1½ in. into the center of the bowl and moving outward to the wall until ¼ in. is left. Repeat this process, leaving ¼ in. at the wall each time.

This method leaves strength and rigidity at the base of the thin wall you are cutting. Do not hollow out the bowl and then try to retrace your steps and thin out the wall. It will be too soft and flexible for cutting.

There is an important difference in technique for hollowing end-grain and face-grain bowls. For an end-grain bowl, after plunging into the center, pull the cut toward you and away from the center. This way, the fibers you are cutting are supported by the fibers behind them, and you are not cutting directly into the grain. For a face-grain bowl, do the opposite. After plunging into the center, start at the outside of the plunged hole and cut away from yourself, toward the center of the bowl.

When nearing the bottom of the bowl, leave only the overall bowl thickness (usually ¼ in.) between the inside surface and the tips of the screws used to mount the bowl. Later, when hollowing the bottom of the bowl, go just far enough to turn out the screw holes, and the bottom thickness will be right.

After turning the bowl, allow the surface to air-dry before sanding. Leaving the bowl on the faceplate for a day is usually sufficient, depending on conditions, but a few hours might do in hot, dry weather. If you power-sand, as I do, put the lathe on a slow speed and don't apply too much pressure in one area. Any heat buildup will cause the bowl to crack. Wet-sanding is also fine, especially if you don't have time to air-dry the bowl's surface.

I like to leave a foot on the bottom of my vessels. To finish this type of bowl, jam- or reverse-turn the screw holes out of the bottom and hollow out the foot, continuing the uniform wall thickness into the foot as shown on p. 132. For a round bottom, you just turn off the bowl with a parting tool. Don't power-sand the bottom; it is prone to cracking and should be left until the bowl is completely dry.

Turning the bowls: Face grain versus end grain

Today's long, heavy, deep-fluted bowl gouges slice easily through green wood, with thick shavings streaming off the blank. The shearing action leaves bark edges intact and works well on interrupted cuts, such as when the blank is being roughed. A note of caution for green wood: Work your way out to the thin wall and then leave that edge alone as you move deeper into the bowl. Returning to a thin edge turned previously is dangerous because it already will have started to dry and move.

FACE GRAIN

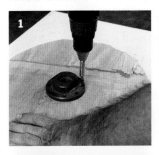

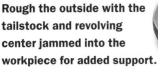

Rough the outside with the tailstock and revolving center jammed into the workpiece for added support.

1. Use a faceplate to mount green wood on the lathe. Other mounting devices won't grab the soft, wet fibers as well. When turning, be careful to direct the cut with the grain, not against it; otherwise, the fibers will tear out and may catch the tool.
2. For the outside of face-grain bowls, as is the case here, the cuts are pushed from the center and bottom toward the outside and top of the bowl (left to right).
3. For hollowing, the tailstock is pulled out of the way. After a small plunging cut is made at the center, each successive cut begins at the outside edge of the last cut and moves in toward the center.
4. Leave ¼ in. of wood at the wall, then begin the next series of cuts at the center again and work out to the wall, and so on.

END GRAIN

Cuts are made in the opposite direction for end-grain vessels.

1. Outside roughing cuts move from the rim of the vessel toward the bottom, here from right to left.
2. Then the tailstock is pulled away, the tool rest is reoriented, and hollowing cuts are plunged in at the center and pulled back toward the wall.
3. When ¼ in. of wood is left at the wall, the next cut begins at the center again, and so on.
4. With today's sharper, longer gouges, scrapers are not needed for the final cut on any surfaces. A planing cut, made with the tool's bevel riding along the surface just cut and acting as a lever point, leaves an even surface for sanding.

Finishing up

The bowl is sanded while still on the faceplate, then the faceplate is removed and the bowl is reversed and mounted on a jam chuck for turning the foot. Controlled drying comes next, then a final light sanding before finishing.

SANDING

Give the bowl about a day to air-dry before sanding it. If you choose power-sanding, don't linger too long in one area or the bowl will heat up and crack in that spot.

REVERSE-TURNING

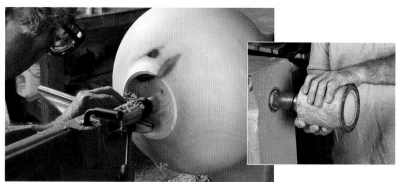

A jam chuck is screwed on for reversing the mounting position and turning the foot of the bowl. A hardwood block with a rubber foot attached makes an effective jam chuck. Turn the foot until the screw holes disappear. At that point, the bottom of the bowl and the sides of the foot should be the same thickness as the wall. This uniform thickness will allow the bowl to relieve stresses as it dries, preventing cracks.

The trick to drying

Place the wet bowl into three brown supermarket bags, one inside the other, and wrap each tightly. If your area of the country is drier or more humid, three bags may be too many or too few. I've found Los Angeles to be a three-bag town (there's a joke there somewhere). Do not use plastic bags. Check the bags periodically. When the bags are bone-dry, the bowl is dry. That's it. The bags slow the drying process, allowing moisture to leave the bowl slowly. This process can take anywhere from one or two days to three weeks, depending on location, season, and wall thickness. If you have chosen your bowl blanks for movement, as I often do, mysterious events take place inside these brown bags.

Another drying technique is to nuke the bowl in a microwave oven. However, a microwave can't vent moisture well, so you will have to make many trips to the oven, giving the bowl one-minute bursts on the high setting, and taking it out each time to let off steam. I can accomplish the same thing with paper bags without any of the effort. The upside to microwave heating, is that you can bend the hot, thin walls toward each other, for example, like a pitcher. You will have fun explaining how you turned the bowl this way.

Here's the bottom line

Cut your blank out of a green log, the wetter the better. Turn the whole bowl in one session, keeping the wall thin and uniform. Sand lightly. Allow the bowl to dry in paper bags, sand lightly again, if necessary, and apply a finish. That's it. The true test is to go out to your shop and try it. The wood is free, and the design possibilities are endless.

Turning Wooden Boxes

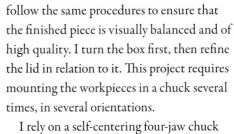

RICHARD RAFFAN

Even after 35 years as a professional wood turner, I never tire of making lidded boxes, perhaps because the round, small containers still offer infinite design challenges.

I find inspiration for boxes everywhere I look, in natural and man-made things. This box is very architectural, a walled structure topped by a roof, or lid, with an overhanging lip and a cupola for a knobby handle. However, boxes can be almost any shape and size, from highly decorated to remarkably simple. The walls can be monumentally thick or ultrathin. And it is not mandatory that the internal form reflect the exterior shape.

No matter what design I pursue, I always follow the same procedures to ensure that the finished piece is visually balanced and of high quality. I turn the box first, then refine the lid in relation to it. This project requires mounting the workpieces in a chuck several times, in several orientations.

I rely on a self-centering four-jaw chuck with dovetail jaws. The jaws fit into shallow grooves that I cut in the wood. The grooves allow me to pop the turning off and on the lathe as many times as necessary, and they also hide the minimal marks left by the serrated jaws.

Start with the box

The lidded box is a faceplate project, with the grain at 90 degrees to the lathe axis. I often cut a pair of blanks for the box and lid from the same 2-in.-thick seasoned block of wood.

Mount the box on the lathe (see the photos on p. 134), true the blank, and square the base to the side. Then turn the base to completion. It needs a foot around the perimeter and a slightly recessed center so that the final box will sit only on the foot. The best tool for cutting the recess is a small scraper with the face and left edge sharpened.

I like to add some decoration to the base. In this case, I rolled two beads with a shallow gouge. Then I sanded the base and added a coat of finish.

Next, remove the center-screw chuck from the lathe and replace it with the four-jaw

Turn the bottom

Mount the blank for the box on a screw-center chuck. Turn the blank to a straight cylinder and then finish the base. Make a recess with angled sides for the four-jaw dovetail chuck to grip later. Finally, sand and apply a finish to the base surface only.

Drill a center hole in the workpiece. Use a drill bit of a slightly smaller diameter than the screw projecting from the chuck.

Mount the turning blank on the lathe. A plywood spacer prevents the center screw from driving too deep into the workpiece.

Begin at the bottom. After smoothing the blank into a cylinder, cut a 3/32-in.-deep recess in the base. It not only looks nice; it gives the chuck a place to grip.

Finish off the base. Add a few details with a shallow gouge, then sand and finish.

chuck. Mount the box on the chuck and finish turning its profile. I prefer a 3/8-in. shallow gouge with a long fingernail grind for working the exterior and turning two beads on the outside, at the base. If you have a problem getting a clean cut on the end grain with the gouge, try shear scraping by holding a round-nose scraper at about 45 degrees to the tool rest. A successful shear scrape will produce thin shavings, as opposed to the dust produced by a standard scraping cut.

With the profile completed, hollow the box (see the photos on the facing page). Plan the depth of the box so that the base will be at least 3/8 in. thick, and then mark the depth by driving a 1/4-in. drill bit into the center of the workpiece while the lathe is on.

Lidded-box cross section

The box and the lid are the same diameter (and height), but the walls of the box taper inward, allowing the lid to overhang. The knob is decorative but also provides plenty of room to grip. The lid should be just undersize, compared to the box, so that it can spin freely and won't stick if the wood expands.

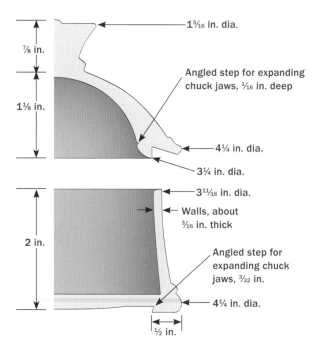

Shape and hollow the box

Mount the box on the four-jaw chuck and tighten it by expanding the jaws inside the angled recess. Then turn the box to completion.

Switch to a self-centering chuck. Remove the box from the screw-center chuck, flip it over, and let the four-jaw chuck hold it.

Drill a depth hole. The center hole lets you know when you've hollowed the box to the correct depth. Leave the base at least ⅜ in. thick.

Turn the outside. Taper the walls to a smaller diameter at the rim so that the lid can hang over the box.

Hollow the inside. Remove most of the waste, cutting from rim to center with a gouge. Keep the walls a consistent thickness.

Square off the inside corner. A round-nose scraper with its edge sharpened to a corner will cut a sharp transition where base and wall meet.

Roll two beads at the base. These decorative elements will complement the overhanging lip on the lid.

Sand and finish on the lathe. Sand with up to P320-grit abrasives, then apply a coat of finish before removing the box from the lathe.

I attached a handle to one of my drill bits so that I can use it like a turning tool with the tool rest. But if you have a drill chuck for the tailstock, you can use that.

With the outside turned and the center hole drilled, hollow the inside using a ⅜-in. deep-fluted bowl gouge, cutting from the rim to the center. When the interior is nearly finished, switch to a ¾-in. square-end scraper with a slight radius to make a nice, sharp corner where the wall meets the base. To limit tearout on the end grain, which makes up nearly 75 percent of the wall, go very

slowly as you make the final cut. If you can't cut cleanly with a scraper, use a ⅜-in. shallow gouge with the bevel rubbing against the wall of the box and the flute pointing to the base. Finally, sand and finish the box, inside and out.

Make the lid to fit loosely

Unlike the box, which is shaped and then hollowed, the lid is hollowed and then shaped. Use the self-centering chuck to hold the wood (see the photos on p. 136). On a turned box of this size, it's unwise to have a tight-fitting lid. Because of the direction of the grain, seasonal wood movement can cause the lid to expand and become jammed in the box. I make the lid so it's just loose enough to spin on the box. The overhanging lip on the lid also helps disguise any movement or distortion that does occur.

Remove the lid from the chuck as needed to see how it looks on the box and to gauge the thickness of the walls. When you're satisfied with the shape, sand and apply a finish.

Make the lid to fit

Mount a blank on the lathe with a center-screw chuck and rough out the outside so that it can be fitted to the four-jaw chuck. Then turn the underside of the lid, checking the fit of the lip with the finished box. Finally, remount the lid and turn the exterior.

Mount the second blank on a center-screw chuck. Turn a round tenon on the end and rough-cut the exterior profile.

Measure the box opening with dividers. Transfer the inner diameter of the box to the lid, which is flipped and remounted.

Use the dividers to scribe the diameter. Dig the left point of the dividers into the work as it is spinning, then see if the right point lines up with the scribed line.

Turn the lip to the scribed line. Check the fit as you work. The lid should fit loosely because the wood will shrink and expand.

Hollow the top. With the lip sized, use a gouge to hollow out the inside of the lid.

Cut a step for the chuck jaws. Similar to the base, cut an angled step on the inside of the lip for the expanding chuck jaws to grab before removing the lid and remounting it. Apply a finish to the inside surface.

Complete the top. Trim the lid and finish off the knob. Then sand and finish.

A Turned Lid from Contrasting Woods

RON LAYPORT

For a dozen years or so I built one-of-a-kind furniture, wrestling giant carcases and tabletops around my shop to the point of exhaustion. I loved the design-as-you-go approach and especially the process of cutting every joint by hand. I was turning down commissions because I was so busy.

Then I attended a workshop to learn to turn my own table legs. That weekend at the Ellsworth School of Woodturning in Quakertown, Pennsylvania, turned out to be a serendipitous miscalculation of monumental proportion. Unbeknownst to me at the time, David Ellsworth was the master of the thin-walled hollow vessel. I spent the weekend learning to turn a bowl and a hollow form, never quite getting to that table leg. I learned that an entire piece can be made, sanded, and finished on the lathe—a far cry from case work. I have yet to build another piece of furniture, and I have never looked back.

Design considerations

My lidded vessels borrow familiar forms from my furniture-making days: beads, coves, elliptical curves. In fact, the overall shape of this vessel is that of a finial. The joinery I use is also borrowed from furniture. If you've ever worked with mortise-and-tenon joinery, you already have an understanding of the banded construction. The contrasting laminations are simply a series of spigots (round tenons) fitted into turned mortises.

I consider pieces like this to be functional art, made to be used. The opening of this vessel is wide enough to allow easy access, and the bottom is a relatively flat french curve.

Required tools and supplies

I used a deep-fluted bowl gouge to form the outside shape. I made the final smoothing cuts with a side-ground gouge that allowed me to lay it on its side bevel for a planing cut.

Though the focus of this chapter is not on turning hollow forms, hollow cutting is necessary to make this vessel. One of my favorite holding devices is the Oneway Stronghold chuck, which has jaws that expand and contract to clamp the inside or outside diameter of a workpiece.

For this piece, I used bigleaf maple burl and ebony. The burl was wet enough to rough out easily but dry enough to minimize distortion later. I got my burl from Mardena Blaney at Exotic Burl (www.exoticburl.com) in Coquille, Oregon. It was difficult to find ebony stock wide enough for the rims on this piece, but resawing, jointing, and gluing up using cyanoacrylate glue and accelerator worked fine.

Anatomy of a lid

The lid consists of contrasting ebony and maple burl parts that are tenoned and mortised into each other. The exact dimensions are not crucial, but the pieces must fit each other closely.

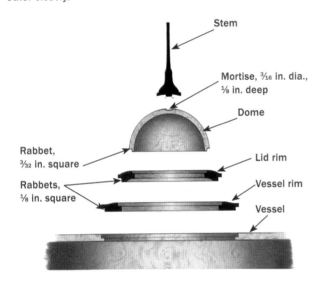

Stem

Mortise, ³⁄₁₆ in. dia., ⅛ in. deep

Dome

Rabbet, ³⁄₃₂ in. square

Lid rim

Rabbets, ⅛ in. square

Vessel rim

Vessel

Shape and hollow the vessel

Start by roughing the general shape between centers. This allows you to reposition the rough blank to avoid or include things like bark or color breaks. True up both ends using

Fit a rim to the vessel. While turning the moist burl, leave extra material at the opening. After the hollow vessel has dried, true up the opening and cut out the small rabbet for the ebony rim.

Mount the ebony blank on a waste block. Glue it at its center only (above left), so it can be parted away later. Turn a rabbeted edge to fit the vessel (above center). Both the outside and inside diameters here are critical. Use the vessel to check the fit (right).

When the fit is right, part away the rim. Then turn a recess in the waste block to hold the rim in the reverse position.

The recess must fit the rabbeted edge. Attach the rim to the block with double-faced carpet tape. Turn the top surface.

Attach the rim to the vessel. Put cyanoacrylate glue on the ebony rim and the accelerator on the vessel.

the gouge, then use a parting tool to turn a ⅜-in. spigot at what will be the foot of the vessel. Next, fit the spigot into a four-jaw chuck to bring the outside of the vessel to its final profile.

I added a flat, wide detail around the opening to create lift and a visual link between the lid and the vessel so that the lid wouldn't appear isolated. Turn the outer edge of this detail to the finished depth, but leave the inner rim about ¹⁄₁₆ in. heavy in thickness

after hollowing. You can go back and true it up after the piece has dried. There is sure to be some distortion on a piece this large and thin, and the opening must closely fit its ebony rim.

I usually put on a coat or two of finish before hollowing, to seal the wood and minimize distortion. Hollow the vessel to a uniform ¼-in. thickness. After hollowing, let the piece dry and settle for several days before truing up the opening. Use the tiniest shearing cuts possible to avoid a catch (and explosion), and clean up the distortion inside the opening with a miniature parting tool. Extreme care must be taken here—this is where I've lost most of these vessels. Lightly sand and refinish this area.

Turn both sides of the rim

Before making the ebony rim for the vessel, cut a ⅛-in. by ⅛-in. rabbet into the vessel's opening. I used a small shop-ground cutter. This rabbeted edge will receive the band of ebony.

Next, glue up a block of ebony for the rim and rough out the circle on the bandsaw. Glue the blank onto a waste block, which goes on a faceplate. If you glue on the ebony only at the center, the ring can be parted easily off the waste block. Turn the stock to about ½ in. thick and trim the outside to fit the rabbet. It must fit without being forced yet without any play. Next, cut a rabbet in the rim so that it will fit into the mouth of the vessel. I use trial-and-error fitting rather than calipers, removing a hair at a time until the pieces slide together.

When this is done, part off the rim and turn an exact recess for the rabbeted shoulder into the same waste block. This recess will hold the rim in the reverse position for turning its other face. To secure rings like this, I use six or eight strips of double-faced carpet tape. The carpet tape is stickier and more substantial than regular double-faced tape. Get an easy, slide-in fit, then add the tape strips, which will jam the workpiece in place.

Trim the center of the rim, then shape the outer surface into a shallow cove that will stand a hair proud of the vessel. Last, trim this inlay band with another rabbet to receive the lid. Sand and finish it, but don't install this fragile rim on the vessel yet, to avoid breaking it with the Stronghold jaws.

Flip the vessel onto the Stronghold chuck, using the jumbo jaws to hold it along the inside of the rim. With the tailstock and a cup center brought up lightly to minimize chatter, shape the bottom, continuing the French curve and using the foot treatment of your choice. I turned the spigot smaller and attached an ebony foot. Sand and finish the bottom. Now you can glue on the vessel's rim and foot.

Turn the lid parts. First, turn another ebony rim. Rabbet it on the bottom to fit the vessel's rim, and rabbet it on the top surface to fit the burl dome to follow. Then turn the decorative elements on the top surface. Leave the rim on its faceplate and waste block.

Turn the small burl dome. While roughing the outside, leave a spigot to hold it for hollowing. After hollowing, turn a precise rabbet on the edge to fit the ebony rim (center above). Mount the dome on the rim and turn a small mortise for the stem (above).

The ebony stem is a spindle turning.
First, turn the bottom of the stem at the tailstock end, working around the live center to turn a spigot and a concave face to fit the burl dome (left). Then part away the stem near the headstock, leaving enough waste to support a center. Mount it on the lid and finish the tip (above).

Turn and fit the lid to the vessel

To make the lid, start with a matching ebony rim to fit the rim on the vessel's opening, using the steps described previously. I don't always add this second ebony rim, but it's a nice touch, disguising the joint between the lid and the vessel. Once this rim fits the rabbet in the vessel's rim, part it away from the waste block. Flip it over, remount it, and make the top surface slightly curved to add visual lift. Clean up the center and cut a $\frac{3}{16}$-in.-deep rabbet to receive the domed burl portion of the lid. Leave the rim in place on its waste block and faceplate.

The burl dome is just a small bowl. Mount it on a faceplate and turn the outside first, leaving a spigot on the bottom. Grab the spigot in a chuck and hollow the dome to $\frac{3}{16}$ in. thick. Turn a rabbet on the outside edge to fit the recess on the inside of the lid's rim. Slightly undercut the shoulder for a tight fit.

Glue the dome onto the lid rim and part away the spigot. Cut a mortise for the stem and give the piece a coat of finish on all but the very top. Set the partially assembled lid aside (still on its waste block and faceplate) to await the stem.

A stem tops off the finial form

Start the ebony stem with its base at the tailstock, and work toward the headstock, turning the thinnest areas last. At the base, create a shallow cup shape to match the curvature of the dome and leave a small spigot in the center to match the mortise. Turn as much of the stem as possible, then part it off near the headstock and glue it into the dome. Remount the entire lid and bring up the tailstock. Perfect the tip of the stem and part away the waste.

Add a final coat of finish to the vessel and the lid. I usually buff a high-end vessel like this, working through the compounds from tripoli to white diamond and ending with a coat of wax.

Turn a Pad-Foot Leg

JON SIEGEL

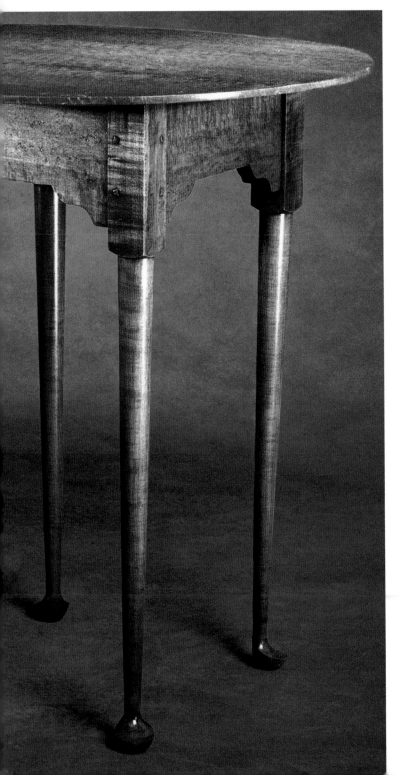

There are many names for the furniture leg that's less elaborate than a cabriole but more complex than a simple taper. I've heard it called pad foot, spoon foot, and Dutch foot. By any name, it was most popular on Queen Anne tables and lowboys. It also can complement Federal or Shaker-inspired furniture.

Unlike cabriole legs, pad-foot legs are produced entirely on the lathe, with no bandsaw work beforehand or hand-finishing afterward.

Making a pad-foot leg involves multi-axis turning—that is, using two pairs of center points. The leg is partially turned while mounted in one pair of centers, then moved to the second pair to finish.

One pair falls at the true center of each end of the leg blank. The second pair is offset in from the true centers in two directions by a fraction of an inch at the bottom of the leg, and a smaller fraction at the top. The two axes—that is, the imaginary lines connecting the centers—cross at a transition point. That's usually at the base of the pommel, the square section that receives the mortises for a table apron or the carcase of a chest.

Accurate layout is critical

To produce these legs, you must precisely locate the two sets of center points and the transition point. That involves careful marking and a little arithmetic.

Start with careful layout

The most important step in turning a pad-foot leg is locating the offset centers on the blank. It's easiest to begin with the offset at the foot, then mark the offset at the top.

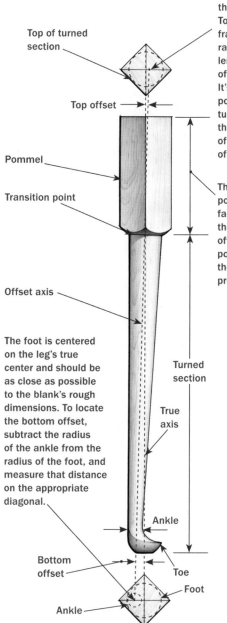

Top of turned section

Top offset

Pommel

Transition point

Offset axis

The foot is centered on the leg's true center and should be as close as possible to the blank's rough dimensions. To locate the bottom offset, subtract the radius of the ankle from the radius of the foot, and measure that distance on the appropriate diagonal.

Turned section

True axis

Ankle

Bottom offset

Toe

Foot

Ankle

The offset at the top is a fraction of the bottom offset. To determine the fraction, calculate the ratio of the pommel length to the length of the turned section. It's 1 to 3 for a 6-in. pommel and an 18-in. turned section. So, in that example, the top offset will be one-third of the bottom offset.

The length of the pommel is one factor in determining the location of the offset centers. The pommel also affects the leg's overall proportions.

Mark the pommel. This defines the transition line where the two axes intersect. Marking all four faces will help you see the line when the leg is turning.

Mark the bottom offset. Measure from the true center toward the inside corner of the leg.

Mark the top offset. Measure from the true center along the diagonal pointing to the outside corner of the leg for this offset point.

For the leg shown here, begin with 8/4 stock, milled to about 1⅞ in. square. (I prefer maple, but any hardwood will do.) A blank that size will give you a well-proportioned leg for many tables. The leg will measure 1¾ in. dia. at the widest part of the foot (that's the line defining the toe), and ¾ in. dia. at the ankle, where the leg is narrowest. The square pommel can be whatever length suits your design.

To find the true center at each end of the blank, I normally use a marking gauge, but for these legs I use a center square because it gives me diagonal lines for the next stage of layout. Don't just connect opposite corners, because that method is not accurate enough. If you use the center square at each corner, the lines will create a tiny square in the center. Punch a hole in the center of this square.

Next, evaluate the appearance of each of the faces, and choose the outside corner where the best faces meet. Make a distinct mark for reference on the inside corner; that will help you orient the offset centers.

To locate the offset centers, you need to know two radii (for the ankle and the foot) and two lengths (for the square pommel and the turned section).

To calculate the offset at the bottom of the leg, subtract the radius of the ankle from the radius of the foot. Measure that distance from the true center along the diagonal pointing to the inside corner, and punch a hole.

The offset at the top of the leg will be a fraction of the offset at the bottom. The fraction is the ratio of the pommel length to the turned length. That is, if the pommel is 6 in. and the turned section 18 in., the ratio is 1 to 3. That means the top offset will be one-third the length of the bottom offset. Measure from the true center along the diagonal pointing to the outside corner and punch another hole.

Shape the leg

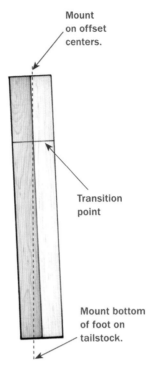

Mount on offset centers.

Transition point

Mount bottom of foot on tailstock.

Begin on offset centers. Most of the leg will be turned with the blank mounted askew. The bottom of the leg, with the greatest offset, goes on the tailstock.

Cut a shallow V-groove at the transition point.

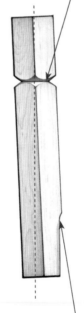

Round one corner and mark the location of the foot.

Cut the transition and mark the foot. Using a skew (above left), cut a V-groove and slightly round the corners of the pommel. Next, you'll need to rough the foot area a bit to round one corner. Stop just short of the inner shadow line; the author is pointing to the spot you want (above right), about ⅛ in. above the second shadow line. Now you can mark a line (right) for the height of the toe.

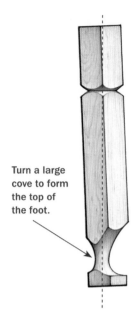

Turn a large cove to form the top of the foot.

Watch the lines. A large cove cut forms the ankle and the top of the foot. Enlarge the cove until you reach the line marking the height of the toe.

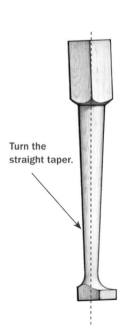

Turn the straight taper.

Cut the taper. When cutting, use your free hand to steady the blank. Check the line with a straightedge.

Finally, draw a dark pencil line to mark the length of the pommel and locate the transition point for the turning. If you mark all four faces of the leg blank, it will be easier to see the transition point when the blank is turning on the lathe.

Begin turning on the offset centers

Mount the blank on the offset center points, with the top of the leg at the headstock. Start the lathe and look carefully at the shadow lines—the multiple images you see as the blank spins eccentrically. Be sure there's only one shadow line at the transition point—the mark you made for the length of the pommel. To tweak the alignment, shut off the lathe and tap the blank near one end to shift it slightly on its centers. Be sure to tighten the blank again so it won't wobble.

Use a ⅝-in. skew with its long point down to make the transition cut. Cut about ⅛ in. to ¼ in. deeper than the flats on the square pommel.

Move to the foot, where you'll see two shadow lines. Use a ¾-in. roughing gouge to cut down to within ⅛ in. of the second shadow line. Because the blank is turning off-center, you'll round off only one corner. Mark a line to locate the height of the foot.

Next, use a ⅝-in. or ½-in. spindle gouge to shape the curve that forms the ankle and the flare at the toe. Begin these cuts well to the left of where you want the toe and widen the curve as you make it deeper. Use calipers to check the diameter at the ankle.

Finally, use the roughing gouge to taper the leg from transition to ankle. Steady the blank with your free hand as you cut, a technique that also allows you to feel any irregularities in the taper. Use a straightedge to check that the taper is even when you make the final smoothing cuts. When this part of the turning is completed, sand it

Finish the foot

Mount on true centers and shape the bottom of the foot.

Mount on true centers.

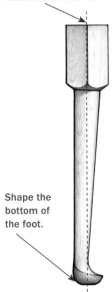

Shape the bottom of the foot.

Complete the turning. With the leg remounted on the true centers, use a spindle gouge to round over the bottom of the foot (left), leaving the diameter at the base ¾ in. to 1 in. Sand the turning lightly (right), being careful to avoid rounding over the sharp line defining the toe.

before going on to the next step. I like to use broken P100-grit and P120-grit sanding belts for the first pass, then finish to at least P220-grit.

Finish on the true centers

Mount the blank on the true centers. Use the ½-in. spindle gouge to shape the bottom of the foot, beginning at the toe. It's the same kind of cut you'd use to shape a bead. Round that part of the leg down so that it's between ¾ in. and 1 in. dia. at the very bottom.

Lightly sand the foot, being careful not to blunt the sharp line that defines the toe.

If you've done everything correctly, that sharp line should blend smoothly into the taper at the back of the leg. If you see a bulge instead of a smooth taper, you can turn or sand it away, although that will reduce the diameter of the toe slightly.

Variations

Sample legs from Siegel's shop (below right) show the range of design options. Siegel's porringer table (below left) adapts one of those styles to a Queen Anne design. The legs are splayed slightly to compensate for the angle of the offset.

Barley-Twist Candlesticks

ERNIE CONOVER

Of all the things I make on the lathe, one of the most eye-grabbing is the barley-twist candlestick, which owes its name to a type of English candy traditionally made with a twist. Whether on a dining-room or a kitchen table, the candlesticks, usually made in right- and left-twist pairs, never fail to be the center of conversation, with woodworkers and non-woodworkers alike wondering how they are made. Although one would think that such work must require a router and complicated jigs, the design predates the router by at least 300 years. A lathe and a few simple tools are all you need.

This is a good project for novice turners, as the only turning is where you bring the blank to shape. The spirals are cut entirely by hand, with the lathe used as a vise to hold the work.

Besides a lathe you need some sharp gouges: I use a #9-7 mm (#9 sweep, 7 mm wide), a #9-15 mm, a #7-20 mm, and a #8-18 mm. Gouges close to these in sweep and size would work as well.

Choose wood that is easy to carve. Mahogany (shown) is a good choice for your first try; walnut is durable and looks good on a dining table; basswood is easiest to carve and looks fine in a less-formal setting; and oak was a common choice in 17th-century England.

Prepare the blank and lay out the twists

Before you turn the blank to the cylindrical pattern and drill out the center, be sure to imprint drive-center marks on both ends so that you can chuck the work in the same exact position at either end for carving. When creating the turning, put a gentle cove

Turn a cylinder and lay out the spirals

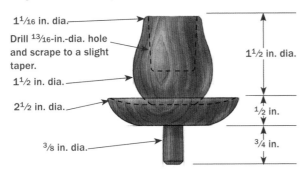

1¹/₁₆ in. dia.

Drill ¹³/₁₆-in.-dia. hole and scrape to a slight taper.

1¹/₂ in. dia.

2¹/₂ in. dia.

³/₈ in. dia.

1¹/₂ in. dia.

¹/₂ in.

³/₄ in.

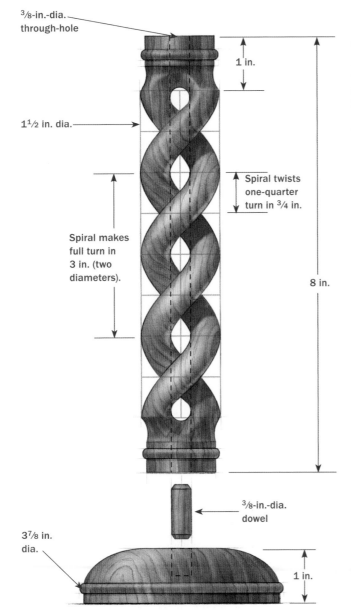

³/₈-in.-dia. through-hole

1 in.

1¹/₂ in. dia.

Spiral twists one-quarter turn in ³/₄ in.

Spiral makes full turn in 3 in. (two diameters).

8 in.

³/₈-in.-dia. dowel

3⁷/₈ in. dia.

1 in.

Lay out the lines. Divide the blank into quarters, marking two opposite lines with a dot to designate where the spirals will start. Then draw lines ³/₄ in. apart around the cylinder.

Draw the spirals. Wrap masking tape around the cylinder, connecting the intersections of the horizontal and circular lines, and mark the line. Do this for both spirals.

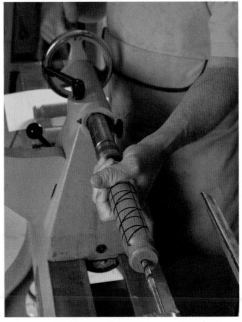

Center-drill the cylinder. Drill the blank from each end to keep the hole centered.

just inside the bead at each end to allow an easy start and finish with the gouges when carving the threads.

The next task is the layout lines. If your lathe has indexing, then use it to draw the four horizontal lines, but you can also use dividers or the lines drawn earlier on the end grain to find the center. Now divide the shaft into ¾-in.-long segments, holding a pencil against the work to create a series of circles.

Although our forefathers would have used a piece of string to lay out the spiral, masking tape does a better job. Wind the tape in a left or right spiral so that one edge crosses each intersection of the 90-degree lines and circles. Repeat for the other spiral.

The next step is to center-drill the blank. For the 1½-in.-dia. column on this design, drill a ⅜-in. hole. Drill from both ends to ensure better centering of the bore.

Saw, carve, and sand the spirals

Use a backsaw to cut a ¼-in.-deep kerf following the curve of the cylinder on the spiral lines you just laid out. Place the #9-7 mm gouge on the tool rest, just as if you were going to make a sheer cut with a turning tool, but skewed to follow the line of the kerf. You want to cut to the right side of the sawkerf to be cutting downhill with the grain. Now turn the work with the lathe's handwheel or an auxiliary wheel (see the drawing on p. 150). If you have the tool at the correct angle, you'll automatically follow the spiral, but if not, simply correct on the fly.

Now reverse the piece end-over-end on the lathe and carve the other side of the kerf, blending in the middle as much as possible. Come back and repeat both cuts using a #9-15 mm gouge to widen the channel.

When you have cut to the bottom of the kerf, deepen the sawkerf and repeat the process. Before you break through to the drill

Twist: Not too loose, not too tight

This barley twist consists of two threads cut into a cylinder. The tightness or looseness of the twist is determined by the length of cylinder covered by each revolution of the spiral. I have found that a spiral that completes one turn in two outside diameters works best. With these three candlesticks, the one on the right has too much twist; the one on the left has too little, whereas the center one looks about right.

hole and weaken the workpiece, use a #7-20 mm or #8-18 mm gouge inverted to round over the top edges of the grooves.

The breakthrough to the drill hole presents the greatest danger of cracking one of the twists. It is easy for the gouge to become a wedge along the grain line. Reduce this risk in three ways: Clear enough wood from both sides of the groove to keep clearance for your gouge, make only light cuts, and use a rasp when breaking through. If all else fails, a bottle of medium-viscosity Super Glue is a good standby.

Once you have a good gap between the spirals, use a gouge on its side or upside down on the tool rest and carve the inside of the spiral by halves to avoid carving against the grain. If you'll be making a lot of these barley twists, use an in-cannel gouge; having the bevel on the inside of the flute gives greater control. You can find them at old tool sales,

Saw the layout line. Use a backsaw to cut a kerf roughly ¼ in. deep along the spiral lines. Gradually spin the piece by hand as you cut.

Carve the channel. Use a narrow gouge to carve a channel along each spiral. Stay to the right of the sawkerf so that you are cutting downhill and not against the grain. Flip the workpiece to carve the second half.

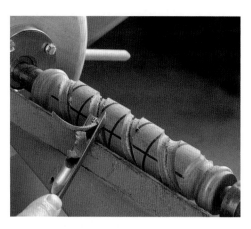

Widen the channel. Come back with a wider gouge to enlarge the channel. Again, always cut on the right side of the kerf. When complete, saw down another ¼ in. and repeat the carving with the narrow and wide gouges.

or regrind an old gouge. You'll need one whose sweep is slightly greater than the diameter of the spiral you're carving.

With the spirals roughly cut to shape, it's time to sand. Because you will not turn the lathe on, it's safe to use cloth-backed abrasive cut into strips. Start with P80-grit and work up to P180-grit paper.

Auxiliary wheel

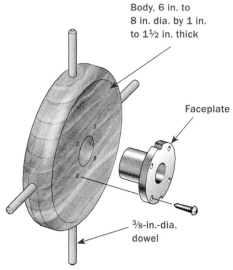

Body, 6 in. to 8 in. dia. by 1 in. to 1½ in. thick

Faceplate

⅜-in.-dia. dowel

An auxiliary wheel makes hand-turning easier.

Round over the spiral. Use an inverted gouge to shape the outside of the spirals.

Saw and carve the spirals

1. Stay to the right of the sawkerf.

2. Flip the blank to carve the other side.

Reveal the center hole and refine the spirals. The workpiece becomes much weaker once you break into the drill hole. To reduce the risks of cracking a spiral, use a rasp when breaking through (above left). Taking light cuts, delicately shape the insides of the spirals (above right).

Work on both sides of the lathe. When cutting a left-hand spiral or certain sections of a right-hand spiral, it is easiest to move the tool rest and work from the back of the lathe.

Turn the other parts and apply a finish

Once everything is sanded to final smoothness, faceplate-turn the base and spindle-turn the candle holder/wax cup. I turn a ⅜-in. tenon on the bottom of the wax cup to glue into the main shaft. I attach the base with a spindle-turned ⅜-in. dowel of the same wood I used for everything else.

Apply a coat of Minwax Antique Oil Finish and sand it in with P220-grit sandpaper. Sanding the wet oil ensures good bonding between coats and forms a slurry of wood dust and oil that fills the pores. When the finish is slightly tacky, wipe it with a clean cloth until almost dry. Repeat the steps with P320-grit, and finish with P400-grit. Aim for a very smooth, glossy surface but not a shiny, plastic look.

Sand and finish on the lathe. With the lathe off, begin sanding the spirals with cloth-backed P80-grit sandpaper. The best method is to tear the abrasive into strips known as shoelaces (top). Wipe on an oil/varnish mix and sand it into the wood to create a smooth, medium-luster finish (above).

Secret to a Sheraton Leg? Divide and Conquer

MARIO RODRIGUEZ

I'm always on the lookout for small but challenging projects, so this Sheraton table caught my eye. It's a stylish piece, compact and delicate. But it was the turned legs that really grabbed me. The top portion is turned to a tight stack of perfectly formed rings. Below the rings are 12 carved, tapered reeds that end neatly in a small ring and reel at ankle height. Under the ring and reel, the leg swells to a smooth bulb, and finally ends in a narrow tip.

All that turning made me hesitate. I've never considered myself a turner, more like a furniture maker who turns a little. So how did I create the four ornate legs you see in the photo? I did it by dividing each one into three separate sections—upper rings, center reeds, and foot—connected by simple mortise-and-tenon joinery. Doing so let me make multiple copies of each section, discarding any single part that wasn't up to snuff without losing the rest of my work.

This safety net also makes the project a great opportunity to grow as a turner. The work can be done on a small lathe, and each section features different details and treatments, requiring a range of skills and techniques.

Straight joints make a straight leg

For this approach to succeed, all the parts must line up correctly: Any misalignment will draw attention to the joints. This means the mortises and tenons must be drilled and turned so they are perfectly straight and concentric with the turned profiles.

For the top and foot, I drill the mortise first and then use it to mount the workpiece on the lathe. In this way, the workpiece rotates around the center of the mortise as the piece is turned. On the middle portion, the tenons are turned with the rest of the workpiece and so share the same centerpoint.

Mortise the top and foot before turning

I begin with the blank for the top portion. I cut away one long corner of the blank, measuring ¾ in. by ¾ in. When the table is assembled, this recess fits around the corner of the case. For now, I fill in the missing section with a piece of scrap and glue it in with thick paper placed between the scrap and the workpiece. This allows me to easily remove the fill-in piece after drilling my mortise and turning the rings, without damaging the top section.

I use a mortiser or a drill press with a right-angle guide and a sharp Forstner bit to drill the mortises. After drilling the mortises, I mount the blank on the lathe by fitting the mortise onto a shopmade mandrel chucked into the lathe's jaws. I secure the other end with the live tail stock.

After turning the blank round, I use a sharp ¼-in. beading tool to mark out and

The **top** section is turned with two sets of rings, grouped to match the width of the drawer faces.

The **center** section is tenoned on both ends. The upper portion begins with a ring that aligns with the bottom of the case. A series of turned shapes gives way to a long, straight taper into which the reeds are cut.

The reeds in the center section die beautifully into the **bottom** section. Another series of traditional details leads to the elongated taper at the foot.

cut clean, exact rings. Afterward, I lightly sand the rings with P220-grit paper and use a handful of shavings to burnish them to a smooth finish.

Although the patterns and dimensions are different, the foot is mortised and turned in essentially the same way.

Two jigs take the risk out of reeding

After roughing the entire center-section blank to a cylinder, mark out and use a parting tool to turn the tenons. To ensure precise diameters and a snug fit, I use open-end wrenches to gauge the tenon thicknesses as I work. This is crucial, as any play in the joinery would definitely affect the appearance and registration of the parts and might cause the joints to fail.

Afterward, turn the pattern of coves and beads at the top, then use a spindle gouge to turn the rest of the piece to a taper measuring 1⅜ in. dia. at the top and ⅞ in. at the foot end.

The top section is notched to join the case

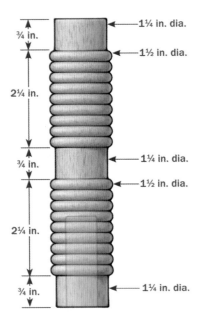

¾ in.
1¼ in. dia.
1½ in. dia.
2¼ in.
1¼ in. dia.
¾ in.
1½ in. dia.
2¼ in.
¾ in.
1¼ in. dia.

Notch the blank. Cut away one quarter of the leg. Then, to make the blank whole for turning, glue in a piece of scrap. A layer of kraft paper makes the scrap block easy to remove later.

Attaching the legs to the case

The corners of the case are chamfered to allow the legs to be pulled tightly to them.

The legs are held in place with screws driven through the case corners at an angle from the inside, a period-correct technique.

The tenon at the top of the center leg section is pared to accommodate the case corner.

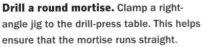

Drill a round mortise. Clamp a right-angle jig to the drill-press table. This helps ensure that the mortise runs straight.

A shopmade fixture holds the work. The workpiece mounts on a mandrel turned to fit snugly in the mortise. The mandrel is held in a chuck. The opposite end of the workpiece is held with a live center in the tail stock.

Turn the rings with a bead-cutting tool. Use the tool to score the outline for all of the rings as a reference before forming them. Afterward, use a sharp chisel to pry away the glued-in filler block.

The center section is tapered and reeded

CENTER SECTION

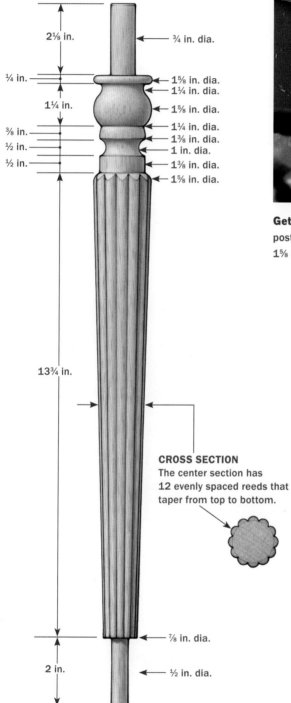

2⅛ in. — ← ¾ in. dia.

¼ in. — ← 1⅝ in. dia.
← 1¼ in. dia.

1¼ in. ← 1⅝ in. dia.

⅜ in. — ← 1¼ in. dia.
← 1⅜ in. dia.
½ in. — ← 1 in. dia.
½ in. — ← 1⅜ in. dia.
← 1⅝ in. dia.

13¾ in.

CROSS SECTION
The center section has
12 evenly spaced reeds that
taper from top to bottom.

← ⅞ in. dia.

2 in. ← ½ in. dia.

Get ready for reeding. Turn the details at the top of this post. Then use a spindle gouge to cut a straight taper, from 1⅝ in. dia. to ⅞ in.

Rout the reeds on the lathe

To cut the reeds, I made a simple jig that supports and guides a router as it travels along the length of the leg (see p. 156). The jig surrounds the workpiece, which remains secured between centers on the lathe. But because the leg tapers, this jig has adjustable tilting guide rails.

With a ¾-in. straight router bit loaded into a trim router, adjust the rails so the router bit just touches the leg at both ends. With both the router and the lathe running, pass the router up and down the length of the leg. This removes any rough spots on the surface and produces a perfectly concentric taper. Now you're ready to reed the leg.

First, plot a cross-section of the leg on a scrap piece of plywood. In this case, 12 reeds fit around the leg. The 12 reeds will be situated with an indexing head built into the lathe headstock. Because the reeds taper, it's impossible to cut full and complete reeds with the router. The best you can hope for is straight partial reeds that you can finish with rasps and files.

Use a point-cutting roundover bit and set it for a light cut. Remember, the smaller diameter at the foot end still has 12 reeds, but they are cut to a slightly shallower depth. Lock the leg into position with the indexing head and cut a single reed, then rotate the leg until all 12 reeds are cut.

A box for reeding. Before mounting the workpiece between the lathe centers, Rodriguez clamps the reeding jig to the lathe bed.

Reeding jig

Anchored to the lathe bed with clamps, the jig is a plywood box with an adjustable-height rail on each wall. The router rides on the rails, which are set above the workpiece, parallel to its taper.

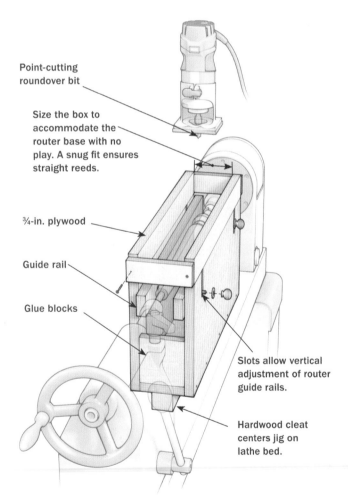

Point-cutting roundover bit

Size the box to accommodate the router base with no play. A snug fit ensures straight reeds.

¾-in. plywood

Guide rail

Glue blocks

Slots allow vertical adjustment of router guide rails.

Hardwood cleat centers jig on lathe bed.

Rout the reeds. Start with a light cut and be sure the jig's rails are aligned properly. Use the lathe's indexing head (above) to lock the workpiece in position at 30-degree intervals. The bit leaves flat-topped reeds (below) that must be rounded (see the facing page) to create the finished appearance.

Bench jig

To hold the workpiece while refining and smoothing the reeds, Rodriguez created this simple jig by mounting a pair of drilled blocks on a piece of flat stock.

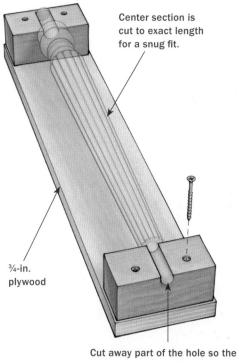

Center section is cut to exact length for a snug fit.

¾-in. plywood

Cut away part of the hole so the tenons snap in place.

Refine the reeds by hand. Rodriguez mounts the workpiece in a shopmade jig, then uses a variety of tools to round the tops of the reeds and sharpen the grooves.

Refine the shapes at the bench

To finish shaping the reeds, I made a bench-top jig to hold the work and provide easy access to the full length of each reed. This is another great advantage of building the leg in three parts: I can shape and sand the reeds straight through without interference on either end. This produces clean, perfect, and smooth results along their entire length.

I use a shoulder plane and detail files to remove the sharp edges of each reed, carefully rounding the tops. Then I use a knife-edge file between the reeds to sharpen and deepen their profile.

For a smooth finish, I use a set of small rubber sanding shapes, changing them frequently to match the taper of the reeds toward the small end.

Create a flat on the tenon. The tenon will be exposed by the cutaway portion of the leg. The flat surface lets the legs marry to the beveled corners of the case.

A graceful foot. Use the shopmade mandrel again to mount the foot blank on the lathe, using the tailstock and a live center again to stabilize the piece. The foot is shaped using a parting tool and a variety of spindle gouges.

Foot

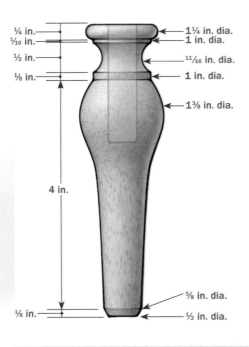

¼ in.
⅛₆ in.
½ in.
⅛ in.

1¼ in. dia.
1 in. dia.
¹¹⁄₁₆ in. dia.
1 in. dia.
1⅜ in. dia.

4 in.

⅝ in. dia.
½ in. dia.
⅛ in.

Mix and match parts before glue-up

After preparing all the leg sections, test the fit of the different parts. Each section should slip in snugly, without any play or pressure at the joint. Sight down the length of each leg; it should be straight and appear as if turned as a single piece. You may find that the mortise in the top section wasn't perfectly drilled, causing the leg to cant in or out of alignment. If so, the cutout corner can be fine-tuned for a straight and square fit.

Another advantage to this method is that it lets you select the best-looking parts for the front legs and put the lesser parts on the back legs. You also can rotate each section for the best appearance, color, and grain orientation.

When you're satisfied, mark the alignments with a pencil tick on a strip of masking tape. Next, take everything apart and carefully cut a shallow notch along each tenon to let excess glue escape instead of pooling in the mortise and preventing the joint from going together. Apply glue to the sides of the mortise and gently slide the sections together. Just before the joint closes, rotate the pieces and align the pencil ticks. If you've done careful work, you won't even need to clamp the leg assembly.

Turn a Classic Floor Lamp

ERNIE CONOVER

As an avid reader, I have long appreciated the good illumination afforded by a floor lamp. Most store models are incompatible with period furniture and tend to be expensive and, to my way of thinking, a bit too low for good over-the-shoulder illumination.

When designing the floor lamp, I looked to the late 18th century for inspiration. A design that originally would have held a candle (hence such vestiges as the cup just below the socket to catch wax drippings) still works well electrified. Building this lamp allows you to practice both faceplate and spindle turning. The base (12 in. dia. by 3 in. high) is faceplate-turned, as is the wax cup. The three spindle-turned feet ensure that the lamp will never rock and allow the electrical cord to exit the bottom of the lamp in any direction.

The design accommodates a range of lathe sizes as well as different turning abilities. Depending on your lathe's distance between centers, you can either turn the shaft in one 36-in. section, as I did, or in 24-in. and 14-in. sections, the extra 2 in. to allow for a tenon. A bead in the main shaft will conceal the joint.

The lamp can be turned from any durable hardwood. I chose mahogany because it was the preferred wood of late-18th-century craftsmen. Also, it is straight grained, so it is very easy to turn and will tolerate generous amounts of scraping.

Prepare the stock

It is easiest to glue up stock for the shaft from two or more pieces of wood. Before glue-up, mill a trough in each half of the blanks with a small core-box bit. Although I do this with a handheld router and a fence, a router table will work just as well.

When I made the lamp, my lumber merchant had sold out of 8/4 and 6/4 mahogany. I therefore had to assemble four pieces of 4/4 stock to create a hollow core. Two pieces of ¾-in.-sq. poplar at both ends keep the four mahogany sections correctly separated and act as points of contact for the headstock and tailstock centers. To avoid gaps, apply strong, even clamping pressure during glue up.

If you prefer to make the shaft from a single piece of mahogany, you will have to drill through the center of the main shaft with a pod auger (often call a lamp auger). This task requires special equipment: You will need either a hollow-tailstock spindle with a special hollow center or an accessory that mounts in the tool base (banjo) and holds the work during drilling.

Ideally the base would be turned from a plank of 12/4 stock 12 in. wide. A more economical method is to use a 6-in.-wide plank of 12/4 mahogany. To maintain uniformity of color, cut the stock in half and glue the two pieces side by side.

Start with the upper section of the base

With the lathe turning at 900 rpm to 1,100 rpm, rough out a 3-in.-wide by 3-in.-deep by 10-in.-long blank with a roughing-out gouge until there are no flat spots. Next, turn a tenon 1¼ in. dia. by 2 in. long using a bedan. To gauge the final diameter use either a pair of calipers or a wrench of the correct size. When turning heavy stock (8/4 or bigger), it is common for the center to have a higher moisture content and hence to shrink a bit once turned. For this reason allow the tenon to dry for a day or two before fitting it to the lower base.

Although some turners recommend using a skew chisel to turn beads (see "Skew Chisels" on p. 4), a spindle gouge is a more forgiving tool. I use a skew chisel to sharpen the profile of a bead by cutting a narrow bevel at its base. Any tearout near the peak of the bulge is sanded out.

When you are satisfied with the surface texture, apply a coat of dark dewaxed shellac (2-lb. to 3-lb. cut). I applied it with a handful of wool from the back of my wife's sheep, but a cotton cloth is nearly as good, if not as exotic. Turn the lathe by hand while applying the shellac. Then burnish the piece by running the lathe at around 1,500 rpm

The base pieces

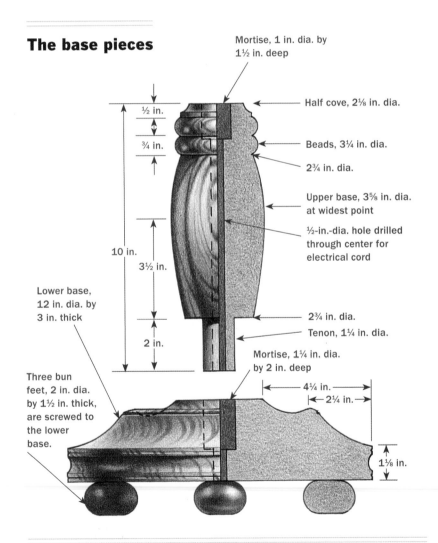

Mortise, 1 in. dia. by 1½ in. deep

½ in.

¾ in.

Half cove, 2⅛ in. dia.

Beads, 3¼ in. dia.

2¾ in. dia.

Upper base, 3⅝ in. dia. at widest point

½-in.-dia. hole drilled through center for electrical cord

10 in.

3½ in.

Lower base, 12 in. dia. by 3 in. thick

2¾ in. dia.

Tenon, 1¼ in. dia.

2 in.

Mortise, 1¼ in. dia. by 2 in. deep

4¼ in.

2¼ in.

Three bun feet, 2 in. dia. by 1½ in. thick, are screwed to the lower base.

1⅛ in.

Turn the upper base first. Cut a 2-in.-long tenon using a bedan. Use a pair of calipers to determine when the correct diameter of 1¼ in. has been reached.

Make the joint between the upper and lower bases. Flatten the area on the lower base, where the upper base will make contact, with a ½-in. bowl gouge to create a seamless joint.

Hollow main shaft. Four pieces of mahogany surround sections of poplar at each end to form a hollow center for the cord. The poplar sections provide contact points for the lathe's centers.

The main shaft

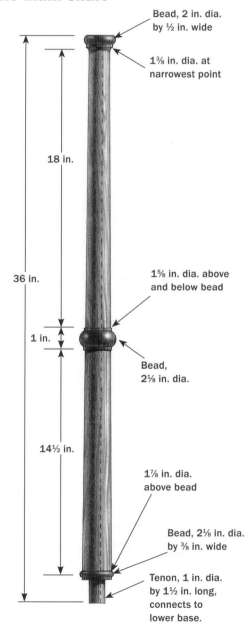

Bead, 2 in. dia. by ½ in. wide

1⅜ in. dia. at narrowest point

18 in.

36 in.

1⅝ in. dia. above and below bead

1 in.

Bead, 2⅛ in. dia.

14½ in.

1⅞ in. dia. above bead

Bead, 2⅛ in. dia. by ⅜ in. wide

Tenon, 1 in. dia. by 1½ in. long, connects to lower base.

Drill through the plug. After the shaft has been turned, sanded, and finished with shellac, drill holes through both solid ends to allow the lamp rod to enter at the top and the cord to exit from the bottom.

Chuck-making scraper

to 1,800 rpm while holding a handful of shavings against the spinning wood. Keep the finish off the tenon to ensure a good glue joint.

Last, drill a ½-in.-dia. hole in from both ends to a depth of about 5 in. Mount a drill bit in a Jacobs chuck held in the headstock. Place the center of the work against the point of the drill and catch the opposite end with the tailstock center. While holding the work to prevent it from spinning, use the tailstock ram to force the work against the drill. Low speed (200 rpm to 300 rpm) is essential. Be sure to back out the drill frequently to eject the shavings and to avoid overheating the bit.

Faceplate-turn the lower base

Mount the blank on a screw chuck and rough it out. Then cut a hole to receive the tenon of the upper base. If you decide to drill the mortise, first mark the exact center of the work using the toe of a skew chisel.

To ensure that the mortise is concentric with the rest of the base, start the cut with a bowl gouge and fine-tune the fit with a chuck-making scraper (see the bottom photo on p. 161). The scraper allows you to cut the mortise to fit the tenon exactly. My tool is a reground ½-in. commercial scraper, but it can be made from an old file or chisel. It is configured so that sharpening keeps the orientation of the edges the same; if the edges were parallel, the left edge would tend to walk across the blank.

For a seamless joint, smooth the area around the mortise to the same diameter as the upper base. Mark the edge of the joint with a pencil to avoid cutting into this area when you turn the rest of the base. Before unchucking the work, apply several coats of shellac, then burnish the piece.

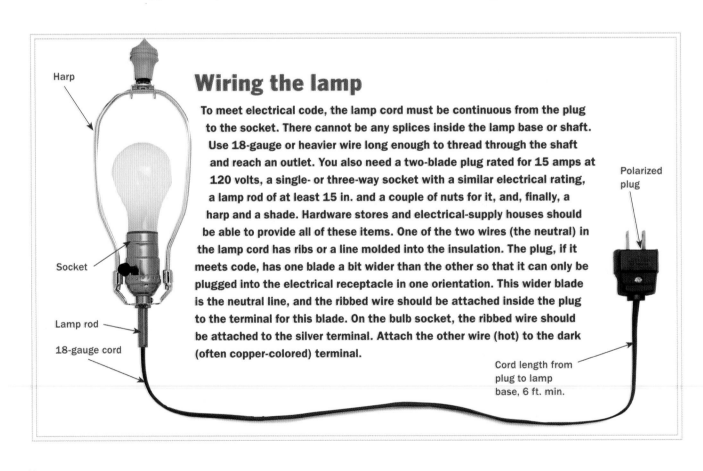

Wiring the lamp

To meet electrical code, the lamp cord must be continuous from the plug to the socket. There cannot be any splices inside the lamp base or shaft. Use 18-gauge or heavier wire long enough to thread through the shaft and reach an outlet. You also need a two-blade plug rated for 15 amps at 120 volts, a single- or three-way socket with a similar electrical rating, a lamp rod of at least 15 in. and a couple of nuts for it, and, finally, a harp and a shade. Hardware stores and electrical-supply houses should be able to provide all of these items. One of the two wires (the neutral) in the lamp cord has ribs or a line molded into the insulation. The plug, if it meets code, has one blade a bit wider than the other so that it can only be plugged into the electrical receptacle in one orientation. This wider blade is the neutral line, and the ribbed wire should be attached inside the plug to the terminal for this blade. On the bulb socket, the ribbed wire should be attached to the silver terminal. Attach the other wire (hot) to the dark (often copper-colored) terminal.

Harp

Socket

Lamp rod

18-gauge cord

Polarized plug

Cord length from plug to lamp base, 6 ft. min.

Now glue the lower and upper bases together, using the pressure of the ram as a clamp, which will ensure that the mating parts are not off center. When dry, drill a 1-in.-dia. hole in the top of the upper base that will receive the tenon of the main shaft. Before unchucking the base, use the lathe's indexing mechanism to lay out three equally spaced locations for the feet.

Turn the main shaft

Rough out the blank, then cut a 1-in.-dia. tenon 1½ in. long at the lower end and a bead just above to conceal it. Roughly halfway up the shaft, another bead breaks up the monotony of a long section and can conceal a joint if you need to turn the shaft in two sections. Before turning the long taper, form the beads to define the diameter of the shaft. To check for a steady taper all the way up the shaft, hold a straightedge to the work. To reduce vibration, steady the workpiece with one hand and guide the tool with your thumb.

Sand the shaft and apply a shellac finish. Then drill a hole through the solid sections at both ends of the shaft to allow the lamp rod to enter at the top and the lamp cord to pass through the bottom.

Turn the last parts and assemble

A 6-in.-dia. by 1-in.-thick blank for the wax cup is turned on a screw chuck. If you do not have one of these, they are easy to make by putting a #8 or #10 wood screw through a block of wood and attaching the block to a faceplate.

The candle blank is 2 in. square and 8 in. long and is turned to imitate a wax candle in its holder. You have the option of painting the shaft a cream color to represent the candle or leaving it in its natural mahogany.

Using the same ⁷⁄₁₆-in. drill bit used to drill the ends of the main shaft, drill down the

Wax cup and candle

The two sides of the wax cup. Turn the piece on a screw chuck and refine the inner and outer surfaces with a scraper.

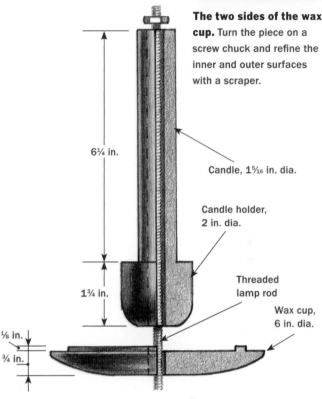

6¼ in.

1¾ in.

⅛ in.

¾ in.

Candle, 1⁵⁄₁₆ in. dia.

Candle holder, 2 in. dia.

Threaded lamp rod

Wax cup, 6 in. dia.

center of the candle section and the wax cup to allow the passage of the lamp rod.

The final items to be turned are the three bun feet made from 2-in. by 2-in. blanks 1½ in. thick. These can be attached to the base using screws or tenons.

With all of the parts completed, dry-assemble the lamp to be sure you are happy with the overall proportions. (I thought the top bead of the upper base was too large, so I decided to reshape that section.) Next, make the electrical connections (see the facing page) and place a suitable lampshade on the harp.

Metric Equivalents

INCHES	CENTIMETERS	MILLIMETERS	INCHES	CENTIMETERS	MILLIMETERS
⅛	0.3	3	13	33.0	330
¼	0.6	6	14	35.6	356
⅜	1.0	10	15	38.1	381
½	1.3	13	16	40.6	406
⅝	1.6	16	17	43.2	432
¾	1.9	19	18	45.7	457
⅞	2.2	22	19	48.3	483
1	2.5	25	20	50.8	508
1¼	3.2	32	21	53.3	533
1½	3.8	38	22	55.9	559
1¾	4.4	44	23	58.4	584
2	5.1	51	24	61.0	610
2½	6.4	64	25	63.5	635
3	7.6	76	26	66.0	660
3½	8.9	89	27	68.6	686
4	10.2	102	28	71.7	717
4½	11.4	114	29	73.7	737
5	12.7	127	30	76.2	762
6	15.2	152	31	78.7	787
7	17.8	178	32	81.3	813
8	20.3	203	33	83.8	838
9	22.9	229	34	86.4	864
10	25.4	254	35	88.9	889
11	27.9	279	36	91.4	914
12	30.5	305			

Contributors

Christian Becksvoort is a *Fine Woodworking* contributing editor and professional furniture maker in New Gloucester, Maine.

Jonathan Binzen is a *Fine Woodworking* senior editor.

Art Breese is a retired engineer living in Sun City West, Arizona.

Jimmy Clewes is a professional wood turner in Las Vegas. Visit him online at www.jimmyclewes.com.

Ernie Conover is a veteran woodworker and author who teaches woodworking at Conover Workshops in Parkman, Ohio. He is also a lathe designer, having developed his own lathe, and worked on the designs of the Nova and the Powermatic 3520b.

Peter Galbert (www.petergalbertchairmaker. com) makes chairs and tools in Sterling, Massachusetts. You can find his blog at chairnotes.blogspot.com.

Kim Carleton Graves designs and builds custom furniture, cabinetry, and wood turnings in Brooklyn, New York.

Barry Gross turns and sells pens, demonstrates pen turning at shows and clubs, and sells pen-turning supplies. For pen-making supplies, visit him online at www.arizonasilhouette.com.

Alan Lacer is a professional wood turner, instructor, and writer living near River Falls, Wisconsin. Visit him online at www.alanlacer.com.

Ron Layport is known internationally for his sculptural approach to the turned wood vessel. His work is included in numerous exhibitions, publications, and collections, both public and private.

Howard Lewin is a retired woodworking instructor and custom woodworker in the Los Angeles area. Visit him online at www.customwooddesign.com.

Philip C. Lowe runs the Furniture Institute of Massachusetts (www.furnituremakingclasses.com). Since 1985 he has operated a furniture making and restoration shop in Beverly, Massachusetts.

Mike Mahoney is a professional wood turner in rural northern California. Visit him online at www.bowlmakerinc.com.

Teri Masachi is a professional woodworker, restorer, and finishing expert who lives near Albuquerque, New Mexico. Visit her online at www.terimasaschi.com.

Richard Raffan is a wood turner and bestselling author living in Canberra, Australia. Look for his most recent book, *Turning Toys with Richard Raffan*, on sale November 2013.

Mario Rodriguez is a longtime contributor who teaches at the Philadelphia Furniture Workshop (www.philadelphiafurnitureworkshop.com).

Jon Siegel is a professional wood turner and toolmaker in Wilmot, New Hampshire.

Bob Smalser is a woodworker and boatbuilder in Seabeck, Washington.

Ralph Tursini is a professional turner and instructor. His training in forestry and woodworking keep him grounded in both his Cambridge, Vermont, studio and local forests. Visit him online at www.vermontwoodturning.com.

Credits

All photos are courtesy of *Fine Woodworking* magazine © The Taunton Press, Inc., except as noted below:

Front cover: Main photo by Patrick McCombe, left photos top to bottom: Matt Berger and Mark Schofield. Back cover from top to bottom: Mark Schofield, Steve Scott, and Mark Schofield.

The articles in this book appeared in the following issues of *Fine Woodworking*:

pp. 4-8: Skew-Chisel Basics by Richard Raffan, issue 145. Photos by Anatole Burkin except for photos p. 5, right photo p. 6, top left photo p. 7, and bottom left photo p. 8 by Michael Pekovich.

pp. 9-16: Scrapers: The Turner's Best Friend by Ernie Conover, issue 208. Photos by Mark Schofield. Drawings by Vince Babak.

pp. 17-21: Gouges for the Lathe by Ernie Conover, issue 123. Photos by Anatole Burkin. Drawings by Jim Richey.

pp. 22-29: The Lathe Accessory Everyone Needs by Ralph Tursini, issue 212. Photos by Patrick McCombe except for product photos by Michael Pekovich. Drawings by Michael Pekovich.

pp. 30-32: Sharpening Gouges: the 40° solution by Mike Mahoney, issue 187. Photos by Matthew Gardner except for photos p. 30 by Rodney Diaz. Drawing by Rodney Diaz.

pp. 33-40: What the Experts Don't Tell You About Turning Furniture Parts by Peter Galbert, issue 231. Photos by Ken St. Onge except for top left photo p. 36 and bottom left photo p. 38 by Kelly J. Dunton. Drawings by Kelly J. Dunton.

pp. 41-48: Learn to Turn Spindles by Ernie Conover, issue 156. Photos by Mark Schofield except for chisel product photos by Kelly J. Dunton. Drawings by Vince Babak.

pp. 49-53: Duplicate Spindles by Hand by Kim Carleton Graves, issue 142. Photos by William Duckworth except for bottom photo p. 49 and left photo p. 51 by Michael Pekovich.

pp. 54-58: Wood Turning: Tips for hollowing end grain by Alan Lacer, issue 177. Photos by Matt Berger.

pp. 59-61: How They Did It: Go beyond the lathe for beautiful vessels by Jonathan Binzen, issue 227. Photos by Brendan Landy. Drawing by John Tetreault.

pp. 62-69: Faceplate Turning is Fun by Jimmy Clewes, issue 218. Photos by Mark Schofield. Drawings by Kelly J. Dunton.

pp. 70-78: Secrets of Segmented Turning by Art Breese, issue 228. Photos by Asa Christiana. Drawings by John Tetreault.

pp. 79-82: Wood Turning: Making split turnings by Philip Lowe, issue 171. Photos by Matt Berger except photos p. 80 courtesy of the North Bennet Street School and photo p. 79 by Kelly J. Dunton. Drawings by Vince Babak.

pp. 83-86: Wood Turning: Fixing turning mistakes by Ernie Conover, issue 169. Photos by Matt Berger.

pp. 87-90: Finish Line: Colorize your turnings by Jimmy Clewes, issue 218. Photos by Mark Schofield.

pp. 91-95: Four Finishes for Turnings by Terri Masaschi 165. Photos by Mark Schofield.

pp. 96-103: Turned Drawer Pulls by Philip C. Lowe, issue 172. Photos by Matt Berger except for photo p. 96 by Kelly J. Dunton.

pp. 104-108: Authentic Shaker Knobs by Christian Becksvoort, issue 196. Photos by Tom Begnal except for photos p. 104, top left photo p. 105, and tool shots by Michael Pekovich.

pp. 109-114: Pens Make Great Gifts by Barry Gross, issue 226. Photos by Mark Schofield except for photos p. 109, p. 110 and p. 111 by John Tetreault.

pp. 115-118: Get a Handle on Your Chisels by Bob Smalser, issue 188. Photos by Steve Scott. Drawing by Vince Babak.

pp. 119-124: Turn a Hollow Vessel by Howard Lewin, issue 154. Photos by Asa Christiana except for photo p. 120, bottom right photo p. 121, and top left photo p. 123 by Kelly J. Dunton. Drawings by Vince Babak.

pp. 125-132: Turning Bowls from Green Wood by Howard Lewin, issue 147. Photos by Asa Christiana. Drawings by Michael Gellatly.

pp. 133-136: Wood Turning: Time-tested method for turning wooden boxes by Richard Raffan, issue 184. Photos by Matt Berger. Drawings by Rodney Diaz.

pp. 137-141: Master Class: A turned lid from contrasting woods by Ron Layport, issue 157. Photos by Asa Christiana. Drawing by Michael Gellatly.

pp. 142-146: Turn a Pad-Foot Leg by Jon Siegel, issue 203. Photos by David Heim except for photo p. 142 by Teri Masaschi and bottom left photo p. 146 by Dean Powell. Drawings by Christopher Mills.

pp. 147-151: Master Class: Barley-twist candlesticks by Ernie Conover, issue 189. Photos by Mark Schofield. Drawings by John Hartman.

pp. 152-158: Secret to a Sheraton Leg? Divide and Conquer by Mario Rodriguez, issue 214. Photos by Steve Scott except for bottom photo p. 156 by Mario Rodriguez. Drawings by Christopher Mills.

pp. 159-163: Turn a Classic Floor Lamp by Ernie Conover, issue 152. Photos by Mark Schofield except photo p. 159 by Erika Marks and bottom right photo p. 161 and photo p. 162 by Kelly J. Dunton. Drawings by Michael Gellatly.

Index

Shaker knobs, 104–8
wooden boxes, 133–36
See also Faceplate turning

Fences, 73

Finishes and finishing, 8,
   91–95
   choosing a finish, 91–92
   lacquer finishes, 94
   oil finishes, 67, 94–95
   preparing the surface,
      92–93
   shellac finishes, 93–94
   sources for, 95
   wax finishes, 93

Floor lamp project, 159–63
   assembling, 163
   bases, turning and finishing,
      160, 162
   dimensions for, 160, 161,
      163
   main shaft, turning and
      finishing, 161, 163
   preparing the stock for, 159
   selecting wood for, 159
   wiring for, 162

Fluting technique, 61

Form scrapers, 15–16

Four-jaw chucks, 22–29
   accessories for, 26–27, 28
   bowls, turning with, 27–28,
      29, 56
   buying, 24
   creating recesses for, 15
   faceplates *vs.*, 29
   hollowing with, 28, 56
   jaws for, 25, 26, 28
   matching to lathe, 24
   securing work with, 24–26
   uses for, 23

Furniture parts, 33–40
   basic tools for, 34
   roughing technique for,
      35–40
   rules for duplicating, 52
   tapers and cigars, turning,
      39–40
   tenons, forming, 40

See also Drawer pulls
   project; Pad-foot
   table legs project;
   Shaker knobs project;
   Sheraton table legs
   project

G

Glue
   repairing with, 83–84,
      85–86
   for split turnings, 79–82

Gouges, 17–21, 30–32
   basic types of, 17
   bowl gouges, 17, 21, 63, 64,
      120–21
   combination gouges, 19–20
   functions of, 17
   high-carbon *vs.* high-speed
      steel (HSS), 17–19
   honing, 21
   in-cannel gouges, 149–50
   profiles of, 19
   roughing out gouges, 17, 18,
      41, 43
   sharpening and grinding,
      20–21, 30–32, 42, 43
   spindle gouges, 17, 19, 42,
      43, 44–48

Grain. *See* Wood grain

Green wood
   bowls, practicing with,
      54–55
   green wood bowl project,
      125–32
   using, for hollow vessel, 120

Green wood bowl project,
   125–32
   advantages of green wood,
      125–26
   cutting blanks from logs,
      126–28, 129
   drying techniques for, 132
   end grain *vs.* face grain
      techniques, 130, 131
   hollowing process for, 130,
      131
   locating bowl blanks, 127,
      128–29

mounting techniques for,
   129
safety tips for turning,
   129–30
sanding and finishing, 130,
   132
turning the outside, 130

Grinders. *See* Bench grinders

Grinding tools. *See* Tools,
   sharpening and grinding

Grinding wheels, 20–21, 43

Grinds, specific types of, 21,
   120

Grooves, cutting technique
   for, 6–7

H

High-carbon steel gouges,
   17–18

High-speed steel (HSS)
   gouges, 19

Hollowing technique, 121–24

Hollow vessel project, 119–24
   boring bar tool for, 119–20,
      121–23
   drying technique for, 124
   green wood for, 120
   hollowing the foot, 124
   hollowing the inside,
      121–24
   shaping the outside, 120–21

Holly veneer, 71

I

In-cannel gouges, 149–50

J

Jam chucks, 132

Jaws, 25, 26, 28

Jigs
   cutting angles with, 71–72
   cutting tenons with, 107–8
   for reeding, 155–57
   for sharpening gouges, 18,
      19, 20, 21, 42

K

Knobs
   drawer pulls project,
      96–103
   Shaker knobs project,
      104–8
   turning, from spindles, 48

L

Lacquer finishes, 94

Lamp project. *See* Floor lamp
   project

Lathes, matching chucks with,
   24

Legs for tables. *See* Pad-foot
   table legs project

Lids
   contrasting wood lid
      project, 137–41
   for wooden boxes project,
      134, 135–36

M

Mandrels, 110

Mistakes, repairing, 83–86
   burn-in stick patches, 86
   flat patches, 83–84
   plugged patches, 84, 85
   replacement beads, 84–85
   sawdust fillers, 85–86
   varying diameter solution,
      83

Mushroom knobs. *See* Shaker
   knobs project

If you like this book, you'll love *Fine Woodworking*.